Sprachtraining
Business English

**Übungen zu Wortschatz
und Grammatik A2 – B1**

Dr. Lutz Walther

Bisher sind in dieser Reihe erschienen:

- Sprachtraining Englisch A1-A2
- Sprachtraining Französisch A1-A2
- Sprachtraining Italienisch A1-A2
- Sprachtraining Spanisch A1-A2
- Sprachtraining Englisch A2-B1
- Sprachtraining Französisch A2-B1
- Sprachtraining Italienisch A2-B1
- Sprachtraining Spanisch A2-B1
- Sprachtraining Business English A2-B1

© Compact Verlag GmbH
Baierbrunner Straße 27, 81379 München
Ausgabe 2018

Redaktion: Sigrid Schulz, Ursula Bachhausen
Fachkorrektur: Patricia McBride
Produktion: Ute Hausleiter
Titelabbildungen: shutterstock: antoninaart (Diagramm), Nikolaeva (Stift),
notkoo (Liste), Olga Tropinina (EU-Flagge), Phant (New York Skyline),
Saint A (PC, Hände, Zeitung, Aktentasche, Wall Street)
Lernkrimi-Logo: Carsten Abelbeck
Gestaltung: PER MEDIEN & MARKETING GmbH, Braunschweig
Umschlaggestaltung: red.sign GbR, Stuttgart

ISBN 978-3-8174-1826-8
381741826/1

www.compactverlag.de

Vorwort

Übung macht den Meister! Mit dem Sprachtraining Business English für geübte Anfänger und Lerner mittleren Sprachniveaus können Sie ganz einfach Ihre Englischkenntnisse verbessern. Abwechslungsreiche und praxisnahe Übungen zu Grammatik und Wortschatz geben Ihnen die Möglichkeit, bereits Gelerntes zu wiederholen oder zu vertiefen.

Die Übungen sind übersichtlich in Wortschatz- und Grammatikkapitel und nach Themengebieten aus dem Berufsalltag geordnet. Aufgelockert wird das Sprachtraining durch anschauliche Fotos und Illustrationen, die gleichzeitig ein bildliches Einprägen sichern. Zudem weisen zahlreiche Infokästen auf Besonderheiten der englischen Sprache hin und helfen Ihnen so, sich in Sprache und Kultur zurechtzufinden und Unsicherheiten zu beseitigen.

Ein leichter Einstieg in die fremdsprachliche Lektüre gelingt mit einem Auszug aus dem Lernkrimi „Manhattan Murder" ab Seite 115. Hier können Sie beim Lesen Ihre Sprachkenntnisse anwenden – und so ganz nebenbei spannend Sprachen lernen.

Die vollständige Geschichte erhalten Sie zusätzlich als kostenlosen Download. Folgen Sie einfach dem Link: https://www.compactverlag.de/download-18268 oder scannen Sie den QR-Code.

Im Anhang finden Sie die Lösungen aller Übungen sowie ein alphabetisches Wörterverzeichnis der englischen Begriffe mit deutscher Übersetzung.

Viel Spaß und Erfolg beim Üben!

Phrasen und Wortschatz ———————— 7

Lernkrimi ———————————————— 115

Anhang ———————————————————— 125

Phrasen und Wortschatz

1 **An introduction.** Welches Wort ist richtig?

Ron: Hi Tracy, how **1.** are / is you today?

Tracy: Hello Ron. I'm fine. How **2.** with / about you?

Ron: I'm fine, too. Tracy, I'd like you to **3.** introduce / meet Ekaterina Krajevna. She's from Ukraine.

Tracy: Hello Ms Krajevna. **4.** Nice / Fine to meet you.

Katya: Nice to meet you, too. But **5.** name / call me Katya, please.

Tracy: All right. Katya, is this your first time in Germany?

Katya: No, as a matter of fact, I've been here before, twice. But I still don't **6.** talk / speak the language. I'm sorry.

Ron: Never mind. We all speak English, don't we?

THIS IS MY NEW COLLEGE ANNA.

2 **Starting a conversation.** Übersetzen Sie.

1. Where are you from?

Von wo kommt du   Woher k...mmen sie

2. What do you do (for a living)?

3. What's your line of business?

Was beschäftigt Sie

4. What sort of company is that?

Welche Sorte von   ist das?

5. When did you arrive?

3 Introducing others. Setzen Sie die Verben ein.

introduce (3x)   introduced   meet   met   name is   this is

1. I'd like you to ....**meet**........ Lucy Austin.

2. Let me ....~~met~~........ you to Lucy Austin.   *introduce*

3. Can I ....*introdce*........ you to Lucy Austin?

4. Have you two been ....*introduced*........?

5. Ben, ...**this is**........ Lucy.

6. May I ....*introduce*........ myself?

7. My ....**name is**........ Lucy Austin.

8. I don't think we've ....**met**........ .   *met*

In der englischsprachigen Welt gilt es als unhöflich, wenn man mit unbekannten Personen zusammentrifft und nicht vorgestellt wird. Auch wenn das Treffen oder Gespräch nur kurz ist, sollte man wissen, mit wem man es zu tun hat. Es ist also wichtig, zumindest den Namen mitzuteilen und eventuell die Herkunft, Abteilung oder Tätigkeit zu nennen sowie die Beziehung, in der man mit der „unbekannten" Person steht.

4 Call me Katya. Setzen Sie die Begriffe ein.

electronics   experience   business relations   management   hospitality

Tracy: Katya, could you say a few words about yourself?

Katya: All right. My name is Ekaterina Krajevna, but please call me Katya for short. I'm

from Kiev, which is the capital of Ukraine. I work as an independent **1.** ....

consultant and was hired and sent here by an **2.** .... company to help

improve **3.** .... between Ukraine and Germany. I'm glad to be here

and would like to thank you for your **4.** .... I'll be staying for

three weeks, which will give us plenty of time to get to know each other and exchange

5. ....

5 Meeting someone. Welche Antwort passt zu welchem Satz? Ordnen Sie zu.

1. [c] Nice to meet you.

2. [d] How are you?

3. [d] Hi, how're you doing? (Am)

4. [e] Hi/Hello. (informal)

5. [b] How do you do? (formal)

a) Fine, thank you.

b) How do you do?

c) Nice to meet you, too.

d) I'm good.

e) Hi/Hello.

Auf den Satz *Nice to meet you.* sagt man beim Kennenlernen
Nice to meet you, too. Geht man nach einer Weile wieder auseinander,
so sagt man *It was nice to meet you.* oder *It was nice meeting you.*
(*Es war nett, sie kennenzulernen.*)

6 Word snake. Finden Sie fünf Dinge, auf die man beim Vorstellen achten sollte.

brownbodylanguagetowerhousepolitenesspizzagesturesforwardpersonalspaceredclothes

7 Saying what you do. Setzen Sie die passenden Verben ein.

involves   work   in charge   do   responsible   report   manage/supervise

1. I arbeiten .... work .... for a large building contractor.

2. I'm leiten .... of all foreign investments.

3. I unterstellt sein .... directly to the managing director.

4. I leiten .... a staff of 20 people.

5. My job zu tun haben mit .... report .... a lot of travelling abroad.

6. I'm verantwortlich sein .... responsible .... for the company's marketing.

7. I machen .... do .... a lot of paperwork and I'm on the phone all day.

8 Having just arrived. Ordnen Sie die Satzteile.

1. at a very   the city centre   nice hotel   not far from   I'm staying
       2   5   3   4   1

2. was okay,   could have   the flight   but the food   been better
       2   4   1   3   5

3. at the airport   thanks for   someone   to pick me up   sending
       5   1   3   4   2

4. jet lag, but   I'll feel better   a bit from   tomorrow morning   I'm suffering
       3   4   2   5   1

5. take a taxi   thanks for   but   I'll   your   offer,   I think
       7   1   4   6   2   3   5

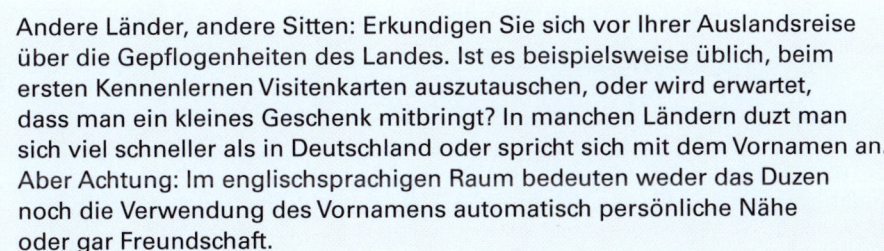

Andere Länder, andere Sitten: Erkundigen Sie sich vor Ihrer Auslandsreise über die Gepflogenheiten des Landes. Ist es beispielsweise üblich, beim ersten Kennenlernen Visitenkarten auszutauschen, oder wird erwartet, dass man ein kleines Geschenk mitbringt? In manchen Ländern duzt man sich viel schneller als in Deutschland oder spricht sich mit dem Vornamen an. Aber Achtung: Im englischsprachigen Raum bedeuten weder das Duzen noch die Verwendung des Vornamens automatisch persönliche Nähe oder gar Freundschaft.

9 Odd one out. Welcher Begriff passt nicht in die Reihe?

1. politeness   courtesy   rudeness   friendliness
2. sleepy   jet lagged   fresh   tired
3. colleague   boss   co-worker   roommate
4. business trip   holidays   journey abroad   travelling
5. hotel   motel   B&B   campsite

10 Introducing guests. Übersetzen Sie die fehlenden Wörter oder Phrasen in der richtigen Form.

Ben: Let me introduce you to our three new members. **1.** Zu meiner Rechten

              ...., please **2.** willkommen heißen ....

              Suzanna Bowline from IRT in Northampton, Massachusetts.

              She **3.** ankommen .... this morning.

Suzan: Hi, great to be in Germany again, but please call me Suzan.

Ben: Suzan **4.** aushelfen werden .... in the finance department.

              She speaks excellent German **5.** übrigens .... And please

              6. begrüßen .... Andrea Caracchini. He's from Rome,

              and he'll be our new marketing assistant this summer.

Andrea: Buon giorno. Hello. Nice to meet all of you.

Ben: And I think you've already met Katya from Kiev. She'll be staying in Martha's office

              7. bis Ende des Monats ....

11 Handshakes. Setzen Sie die Wörter oder Phrasen dort ein, wo sie inhaltlich passen.

exchanged handshakes   on a handshake   limp handshake
warm and hearty   firm handshake

1. The project leader greeted me with a ....

2. We .... and immediately got down to business.

3. She greeted everyone with a .... handshake.

4. Although he's a big guy, for some reason he gives a very ....

5. I like doing business ...., but it's better to sign a "real" contract.

Achten Sie beim Kennenlernen auf den *personal space*, d. h. den Höflich-keitsabstand zwischen zwei Menschen, die sich nicht kennen. Er kann je nach Person und Kultur zwischen 60 cm und 1,50 m betragen. Zwar sollte man nicht zu nah an den Gesprächspartner herantreten, sich andererseits aber auch nicht nach hinten von ihm weg beugen. Zeigen Sie Interesse und Aufmerksamkeit, indem Sie sich leicht zum Gegenüber hinneigen.

12 Being positive. Entscheiden Sie, welche Form richtig ist.

1. Your English is   excellent / excellently . Where did you learn it?

2. From what I've seen so far, your country is   beautiful / beautifully .

3. I'm very   excited / exciting   to learn more about your culture.

4. I'm   positively / positive   that our project will be a success.

5. I'm looking forward to   meeting / meet   the other team members.

6. I'm   interesting / interested   to see more of the company.

13 Answering questions. Übersetzen Sie die Antworten.

1. Ich bin noch nie in Manchester gewesen.

....

2. Ich bleibe drei Tage in London.

....

3. Ich bin gerade vom Flughafen angekommen.

....

4. Das Hotel ist sehr schön und komfortabel.

....

FIRMENTYPEN

1 Types of companies. Ordnen Sie die Definitionen den Firmentypen zu.

subsidiary   corporation (Corp.)   firm   company (Co.)   combine

1. a large company that consists of smaller companies: ....

2. a company that is owned by a bigger company: ....

3. a company that sells a service rather than goods: ....

4. a group of businesses that work together: ....

5. a business organization that sells or produces something: ....

2 More terms. Finden Sie die richtige Übersetzung sowie das Lösungswort.

1. ☐ Global agierendes Unternehmen   **a)** open partnersh☐p

2. ☐ Gewerkschaft   **b)** parent ☐ompany

3. ☐ Familienbetrieb   **c)** private ☐imited company

4. ☐ GmbH   **d)** trade ☐nion

5. ☐ Offene Handelsgesellschaft   **e)** global ☐layer

6. ☐ Muttergesellschaft   **f)** family ☐usiness

Lösung: to go ☐☐☐☐☐☐

Ein an der Börse notiertes britisches Unternehmen nennt man *public limited company* (*plc*). Der Ausdruck *to go public* meint daher den Gang an die Öffentlichkeit, d. h an die Börse. Nicht börslich notierte Firmen tragen meist die Abkürzung *ltd* (*limited*), was bedeutet, dass sie einer beschränkten Haftung (*limited liability*) unterliegen. Die deutsche GmbH entspricht also etwa einer *private limited company*. Die Abkürzung *Inc.* (*incorporated*) verwendet man vor allem für große Aktiengesellschaften in den USA.

3 Business headlines. Vervollständigen Sie die Schlagzeilen.

enterprise   cooperatives   joint   merger   association   takeover

1. Canada and the US agree on a .... venture to build new oil pipeline.

2. Agricultural .... on the rise again.

3. Possible .... between two largest telephone companies.

4. Hostile .... by Chinese company averted.

5. New trade .... to be established soon.

6. Small family business has grown into large-scale ....

4 False friends. Welche Übersetzung ist richtig?

1. Konkurrent   a) ☐ contractor   b) ☐ concurrent   c) ☐ competitor

2. Fabrik   a) ☐ fabric   b) ☐ factory   c) ☐ facilities

3. Lager   a) ☐ hall   b) ☐ warehouse   c) ☐ lager

4. Unternehmer   a) ☐ entrepreneur   b) ☐ actionist   c) ☐ undertaker

5 Business activities. Fügen Sie eine richtige Form des Verbs ein.

1. They to specialize in .... high-tech kitchen equipment.

2. A law firm to provide .... legal services.

3. The company to be founded in .... 1902 by her grandfather.

4. He to sell .... his products on the African market for years.

5. The corporation to always operate .... globally.

6. The subcontractor to employ .... more than 150 people.

7. Cauldon & Sons to be based in .... Manchester.

POSITIONEN UND ABTEILUNGEN

6 Jobs and titles. Fügen Sie die Namen der Führungspositionen ein.

sales manager   managing director   production manager
head of human resources   head of accounting   financial director

Generaldirektor(in)

1. ....

Finanzleiter(in)

2. ....

Personalchef(in)

3. ....

Produktionsleiter(in)

4. ....

Vertriebsleiter(in)

5. ....

Leiter(in) der Buchhaltung

6. ....

7 Positions. Finden Sie sechs Bezeichnungen für Personen in einem Betrieb.

K	W	O	R	K	M	A	T	E	E	O
S	T	A	F	F	M	E	M	B	E	R
T	R	A	C	T	D	E	H	A	W	K
P	A	R	A	X	I	S	M	T	O	A
L	I	N	T	R	O	M	M	A	R	A
I	N	T	E	R	N	E	P	A	K	T
C	E	G	E	M	P	L	O	Y	E	E
W	E	A	D	E	V	Q	U	E	R	A

8 A tour of the premises. Setzen Sie die Namen der Abteilungen ein.

research and development   manufacturing   human resources
public relations   board of directors   sales   accounts

Ladies and Gentlemen: On the ground floor of this building there are lots of offices,

the most important of which is certainly the **1.** .... department, which

deals with invoices, reminders and all company accounts. On the first floor you'll find

the **2.** .... department, where all our press releases are written,

right next to **3.** .... So, if you apply for a job, your application will be

dealt with in this department. Our **4.** .... plant, where everything

is produced, is in the big hall you see over there when you look out of the window.

5. ...., by the way – the creative centre of our company – is also out

there as well as the **6.** .... department, where our products are sold.

The **7.** .... resides on the second floor – they have the best view.

9 A career. Übersetzen Sie die Begriffe.

Theresa McGuire, 32, is vice president of a promising Internet start-up. She was originally

trained as a personal assistant in the **1.** Kundendienstabteilung ....

of a large **2.** Import-Export Firma .... She also worked

in the **3.** Marketingabteilung .... of a prestigious

4. Autofirma .... before she quit her job because she couldn't

handle the **5.** Stress .... anymore. Today, she feels much more

relaxed even though her **6.** Einkommen .... is considerably lower.

ANRUFE ENTGEGENNEHMEN UND WEITERLEITEN

1 A phone call. Bringen Sie den Dialog in die richtige Reihenfolge.

1. Thanks for calling. Good bye.

2. Ah ..., never mind. I'll call back later.

3. Bye.

4. I'm sorry, Ms Jones' line's engaged. Would you like to hold?

5. (*music*)

6. Hello, my name is Sue Allen. I'd like to speak to Ms Jones, please.

7. Jones and Jackson Limited. My name is Carol Baker. How can I help?

8. One moment, please. I'll put you through.

Reihenfolge: ☐☐☐☐☐☐☐☐

2 Phone verbs. Welches Verb passt zu welcher Übersetzung?

1. ☐ to put sb. through   a) am Apparat bleiben

2. ☐ to phone sb.   b) jmdn. zurückrufen

3. ☐ to hold (the line)   c) jmdn. anrufen

4. ☐ to ring sb. back   d) jmdn. durchstellen

5. ☐ to answer the phone   e) jmdn. in der Warteschleife halten

6. ☐ to leave a message   f) eine Nachricht hinterlassen

7. ☐ to put sb. on hold   g) ans Telefon gehen

Die Person, die in der Telefonzentrale eines Unternehmens arbeitet, wird *operator*, *receptionist* oder *telephonist* genannt: ˈɒpəreɪtəʳ / rɪˈsepʃənɪst / təˈlefənɪst.

3 **An urgent call.** Vervollständigen Sie den Dialog mit den angegebenen Wörtern.

to leave   to call ... back   to speak   calling   pass ... on   this is

Receptionist: Jones and Jackson Limited. My name is Randolph Brown.

Caller: Hi, I'd like **1.** .... to Mr Jackson, please.

Receptionist: Can I ask who's **2.** ...., please?

Caller: Ah yes, **3.** .... Fiona Thompson from R&F in Sheffield.

Receptionist: I'm afraid he's in a meeting. Would you like **4.** .... a message?

Caller: Yes, tell him **5.** .... me .... asap.

              He's got my number. It's urgent!

Receptionist: I'll **6.** .... the message .... to him as soon as

              the meeting's over.

Caller: Please do so. Bye.

Receptionist: Thanks for calling. Bye.

> Die deutsche Phrase *Hier ist ...*
> wird im Englischen mit *This is ...*
> oder einfach *It's ...* wieder-
> gegeben. – Die Abkürzung
> *asap* (gesprochen ˈeɪsæp oder
> ˌeɪ es eɪ ˈpiː) bedeutet *as soon*
> *possible* und drückt eine gewisse
> Dringlichkeit aus.

4 **True or false?** Sind die Aussagen zum Dialog in Übung 3 wahr oder falsch?

	True	False
1. The caller wants to speak to Mr Brown.	❏	❏
2. The receptionist's name is Randolph Jackson.	❏	❏
3. Fiona Thompson is calling from R&E in Sheffield.	❏	❏
4. Mr Jackson is in a meeting.	❏	❏
5. The caller does not leave a message.	❏	❏
6. The receptionist will pass on the message immediately.	❏	❏

5 Types of phones. Ordnen Sie die Begriffe den Bildern zu.

hands-free phone   cordless phone   mobile/cell phone

answering machine   vintage telephone   public phone

1. .... 2. .... 3. ....

4. .... 5. .... 6. ....

6 A bad connection. Welcher englische Satz passt zu welcher Übersetzung?

1. ☐ Sorry, I didn't get that.   a) Ich kann Sie fast nicht verstehen.

2. ☐ Can you repeat that, please?   b) Die Verbindung ist sehr schlecht.

3. ☐ I can barely hear you.   c) Tut mir leid, das habe ich nicht verstanden.

4. ☐ Could you call again, please?   d) Können Sie das bitte wiederholen?

5. ☐ The line is very bad.   e) Könnten Sie bitte lauter sprechen?

6. ☐ You've dialled the wrong number.   f) Könnten Sie bitte noch mal anrufen?

7. ☐ Could you speak up, please?   g) Sie haben sich verwählt.

7 Prepositions. Tragen Sie die passende Präposition ein.

on (3x)   in   out   from   at (2x)

1. I'm afraid Mr Barston is .... a meeting.

2. I'm sorry, Ms Baker is not available .... the moment.

3. She's speaking .... another line. Can I put you on hold?

4. They're .... for lunch.

5. I'm sorry, but she's not .... her desk.

6. Mrs Doorley's .... holiday this week.

7. Hi Beth, good to hear .... you again.

8. Carol is not in right now, but you can reach her .... her mobile.

8 Asking questions. Übersetzen Sie die Fragen einer Empfangsdame sinngemäß.

1. Can I ask who's calling, please?

....

2. Can I ask what it's about?

....

3. Could you spell your name, please?

....

4. Would you like to hold?

....

5. One moment, please, I'll put you through.

....

ANRUFE TÄTIGEN UND NACHRICHTEN HINTERLASSEN

9 **Calling somebody.** Wählen Sie die richtige Variante für Ihren Anruf.

1. Could you put me through to the marketing section / department , please?

2. Hello, I'm Oliver Schmidt calling off / from Cologne, Germany.

3. Could you ask / question her to give me a ring this afternoon?

4. Could you take a massage / message , please?

5. Could I have / take extension 310, please?

6. I'll write / fax her an e-mail, then.

10 **Phone phrases.** Welche Sätze passen zusammen?

1. ☐ When would be the best   a) help me.

2. ☐ Could you ask him to phone   b) extension, would you?

3. ☐ I'm calling about the   c) boss, Ms Schmidtbauer.

4. ☐ You wouldn't have her   d) me on my mobile?

5. ☐ I'm phoning on behalf of my   e) new software update you sent me.

6. ☐ I was wondering if you could   f) time to reach her?

11 **To hang up on sb.** Fügen Sie die Verben in die richtigen Lücken ein.

finish   saying   hang up on   rings   answer   put

When the phone **1.** ...., you **2.** .... the phone and say "Hello".

When you **3.** .... a call, you say "goodbye" and **4.** ....

the receiver down. What you shouldn't do is **5.** .... somebody without

6. .... "Goodbye". This is very rude.

12 **Leaving a message.** Bringen Sie die Wörter in die richtige Reihenfolge.

1. is   Mr   message   Thorvaldson   this   a   for

....

2. called   at   I   already   you   five   have   least   times

....

3. cancel   I'm   our   I   morning   to   have   meeting   Friday   on   sorry

....

4. that   please   message   him   on   pass   to

....

5. town   tomorrow   until   afternoon   out   I'm   of

....

6. you   on   should   number   see   display   my   your

....

7. possible   as   get   with   in   me   soon   as   please   touch

....

13 **Prepositions.** Welcher Satz passt zu welcher Präposition? Ordnen Sie zu.

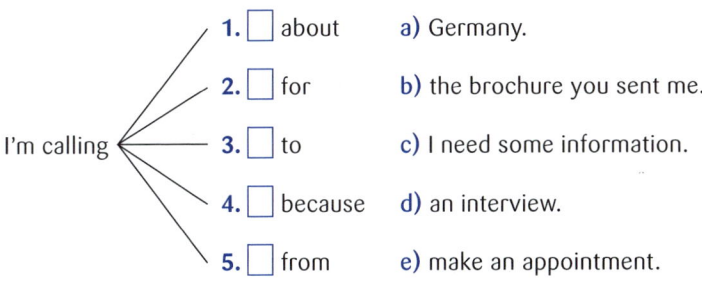

I'm calling

1. ☐ about   a) Germany.

2. ☐ for   b) the brochure you sent me.

3. ☐ to   c) I need some information.

4. ☐ because   d) an interview.

5. ☐ from   e) make an appointment.

Falls man irgendwo abgeschieden auf dem Land sein Mobiltelefon benutzen möchte und kein Netz hat, so sagt man auf Englisch *to have no reception.*

14 Messages. Ihr gewünschter Gesprächspartner ist nicht zu erreichen. Stattdessen hören Sie Folgendes: *This is the voicemail of Spider Ltd. You're calling outside our office hours. Please leave your name, number and a message after the beep.* Finden Sie je einen Fehler in den Nachrichten.

1. My name is Anthony Brackenridge. Please repay this call as soon as you can.

   It's about the invoice (*Rechnung*) you sent me. Thank you very much.

2. It's 5.30! Why isn't there anyone in the office? Here's Mark from R&D.

3. This is a message for Paula. I'm afraid I have to postpone our meeting tomorrow on next

   week.

4. Hello, it's Minnie, expansion 25. I'll try to reach you tomorrow morning.

5. Hi, this is James. Jenny, could you tell Frank that I called and tell him to meet me

   tomorrow afternoon at 4 a.m. instead of 3? Thanks a lot.

6. Ah ..., I was just wondering if you're still being there.

15 Phone words. Übersetzen Sie die Begriffe und Sie finden das Lösungswort.

1. Verbindung ☐ _ _ _ _ _ _ _ _ _

2. Telefonnummer _ ☐ _ _ _ _ _ _ _ _

3. Akku _ ☐ _ _ _ _ _

4. Vorwahl _ ☐ _ _ _ _ _ _

5. Notruf _ _ _ _ ☐ _ _ _ _ _ _ _

6. Durchwahl _ _ _ ☐ _ _ _ _ _

7. kein Netz _ _ ☐ _ _ _ _ _ _ _ _

   Lösung: ☐☐☐☐☐☐☐ (*Ladegerät*)

16 **An impatient caller.** Entscheiden Sie, welche Variante richtig ist.

Receptionist: Cy & Borg Pta., Oscar Marton **1.** speaking / talking .

Caller: Hola, this Anatxu Zuñiga Iñigarai. Can I speak to customer service.

Receptionist: Eh ..., I'm sorry, could you **2.** retell / repeat your name, please?

Caller: Anatxu Zuñiga Iñigarai.

Receptionist: Could you **3.** spoil / spell that, please?

Caller: No time to spell. Speak to customer service.

Receptionist: All right, one moment, please. (*music*). **4.** I'm afraid / I'm anxious all lines

are engaged. Could you call back later, and please dial extension 10.

Caller: No time to call back later.

Receptionist: I'm awfully sorry, Mr ah ..., all lines are busy at the moment. I can put you on

5. held / hold and the next available employee will take care of you.

Caller: Okay, I wait. But please hurry.

Receptionist: Thanks for **6.** dialling / calling Cy & Borg. Goodbye.

17 **Phone numbers.** Schreiben Sie die Ziffern der Telefonnummern aus.

1. 001.781 ....

2. 0044.143 ....

> Telefonnummern werden im Englischen in der Regel Ziffer für Ziffer genannt.
> Stehen zwei gleiche Ziffern hintereinander, sagt man häufig *double*, bei drei
> Ziffern kann man *triple* sagen oder sie einzeln aussprechen; die Null heißt
> entweder *o* oder *zero*. – Die Vorwahl eines Lands heißt *country code*; die
> eines Ortes *city code* oder *area code*.

ANFRAGEN UND ANTWORTSCHREIBEN

1 Types of correspondence. Welche Übersetzung ist richtig?

1. inquiry/enquiry   a) ☐ Bestätigung   b) ☐ Anfrage   c) ☐ Rechnung

2. complaint   a) ☐ Rechnung   b) ☐ Einladung   c) ☐ Beschwerde

3. application   a) ☐ Einladung   b) ☐ Bestellung   c) ☐ Bewerbung

4. invoice   a) ☐ Mahnung   b) ☐ Rechnung   c) ☐ Bestätigung

5. reminder   a) ☐ Anfrage   b) ☐ Beschwerde   c) ☐ Mahnung

6. invitation   a) ☐ Bewerbung   b) ☐ Mahnung   c) ☐ Einladung

7. order   a) ☐ Bestellung   b) ☐ Bewerbung   c) ☐ Anfrage

8. confirmation   a) ☐ Beschwerde   b) ☐ Bestätigung   c) ☐ Einladung

Eine *enquiry* oder *inquiry* [ɪnˈkwaɪəri] (im Amerikanischen auch [ˈɪnkwəri],
ist eine unverbindliche Anfrage nach Informationen, Katalogen, Preislisten
o.ä. Sie ist allgemein, kurz und höflich gehalten und gibt dem Adressaten
die Möglichkeit, relativ unkompliziert zu reagieren.

2 Beginning phrases. Fügen Sie die passenden Begriffe ein.

hoping   grateful   contacting   to enquire   let me know   interested in   if

1. I'm writing .... about ...

2. I was wondering .... you ...

3. I was .... you might be able to ...

4. I would be .... if you could ...

5. I'm particularly .... learning ...

6. Could you please .... if ...

7. I am .... you because ...

3 **Parts of an email.** Benennen Sie die sechs Teile der E-Mail.

introduction   opening salutation   closing sentence
sender's name   closing salutation   reason for writing

To:

Re:

1. Dear Sir or Madam

2. I saw your stand at the Hanover computer fair
   last week.

3. I'm particularly interested in your new spy
   software. Since I couldn't find a price list
   on your website, I'd be grateful if you could send
   me one or tell me the link where I can find it.

4. I'm looking forward to hearing from you.

5. Best regards

6. Tom

Die Abkürzung *Ms* wird für Frauen verwendet, wenn man nicht weiß, ob sie verheiratet sind oder nicht. Alle Abkürzungen werden im Englischen ohne Punkt, im Amerikanischen mit Punkt geschrieben. – Bei *Dear Sir or Madam* steht tatsächlich der Herr vorn. Die Anrede *Dear Sirs*, die ebenfalls beide Geschlechter anspricht, wird heute nicht mehr verwendet.

1. ....   2. ....   3. ....

4. ....   5. ....   6. ....

4 **Opening salutations.** Welche englische Anrede entspricht welcher deutschen?

1. ☐ Dear Mrs/Ms (name)   a) Liebe/r (Name)

2. ☐ Dear Sir or Madam   b) Sehr geehrter Herr (Name)

3. ☐ To Whom It May Concern   c) Hallo (Name)

4. ☐ Dear (name)   d) Sehr geehrte Damen und Herren

5. ☐ Hello (name)   e) *keine Entsprechung im Deutschen*

6. ☐ Dear Mr (name)   f) Sehr geehrte Frau (Name)

5 Closing sentences. Fügen Sie eine passende Präposition ein.

1. Thank you .... your attention.

2. I look forward .... hearing from you.

3. I hope to hear .... you soon.

4. Thanks .... advance.

6 Closing salutations. Ordnen Sie die Grußformeln der Förmlichkeit nach: die formellste zuerst.

Regards   Yours sincerely   Yours faithfully   Love   Best wishes   All the best

1. ....   **2.** ....   **3.** ....

4. ....   **5.** ....   **6.** ....

> Die Formel *Yours faithfully* ist sehr förmlich und wird in E-Mails so gut wie nicht verwendet. Amerikaner schreiben statt *Yours sincerely* auch *Sincerely yours*.

7 Following up. Kreuzen Sie die Phrasen an, die auf eine vorangegangene Korrespondenz Bezug nehmen.

1. ☐ I'm writing in response to your letter of 23 September ...

2. ☐ Further to our phone conversation this morning ...

3. ☐ Following on from our meeting yesterday ...

4. ☐ In reply to your email of 1 August ...

5. ☐ Thank you for your written inquiry ...

6. ☐ I'm writing to you in/with reference to your quotation of 8 May ...

7. ☐ As we discussed in our meeting Friday afternoon ...

BESTELLUNGEN UND BESTELLBESTÄTIGUNGEN

8 Placing an order. Setzen Sie die Begriffe in die E-Mail ein.

goods   payment   offer   order   receipt   company   confirmation   discount

---

To: matsuo@engineering.com
Re: Order electronic parts
Cc: info@it-department

Dear Mr Matsuo

Thank you for your **1.** .... of 13 March 2018. We have decided

to place an **2.** .... with your **3.** ...., accepting

the 15 percent volume **4.** .... you promised to give.

Order number	Amount	Net price per item acc. to catalogue
40 256-B	300	$ 258.00
40 257-D	150	$ 300.00
40 258-A	80	$ 490.00

It is hereby agreed that you will deliver the **5.** .... to our

warehouse in Dublin within six weeks of **6.** .... of this order.

7. .... will be made by letter of credit (L/C). We therefore would

like to ask you to send us a pro forma invoice.

Please send us a **8.** .... of this order. If everything is carried out to

our satisfaction, we are certain that further orders will follow.

We are looking forward to hearing from you.

Yours sincerely

Larry O'Shaughnessy
Purchaser

9 Types of orders. Entwirren Sie die Auftrags- und Bestellarten.

1. Probebestellung   atril .... order

2. Folgebestellung   pereat .... order

3. Abrufauftrag   order no lalc ....

4. Vorbestellung   cevadan .... order

5. Eilauftrag   suhr .... order

6. Dauerauftrag   dinstang .... order

10 Abbreviations. In E-Mails werden häufig Abkürzungen verwendet. Was bedeuten sie?

	Englisch	Deutsch (ggf. mit Abkürzung)
1. re.	....	....
2. FYI	....	....
3. P.A.	....	....
4. e.g.	....	....
5. FAO	....	....
6. i.e.	....	....
7. no.	....	....
8. approx.	....	....
9. c/o	....	....

Die ebenfalls häufig verwendeten Abkürzungen *a.m.* (*ante meridiem*) und *p.m.* (*post meridiem*) verwendet man für Urzeiten vor- und nach dem „Mittag": a.m. = 0 Uhr bis 11:59 Uhr; p.m. = 12 Uhr bis 23:59 Uhr.

11 Confirmation of order. Bringen Sie die E-Mail in die richtige Reihenfolge.

1. We look forward to hearing from you soon.

2. We would also like to tell you that the consignment is going to be dispatched next Monday.

3. Best regards, Hiroka Nishikawa (P.A. to Akio Matsuo)

4. We confirm the receipt of your order of 300 items
40 256-B, 150 items 40 257-D and 80 items 40 258-A.

5. Dear Mr O'Shaughnessy

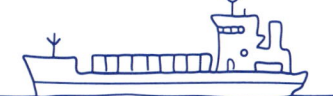

6. As promised you will get a 15% discount on your purchase, and we will send you
a pro forma invoice by return.

Reihenfolge: ☐ ☐ ☐ ☐ ☐ ☐

12 An apology. Welche Variante ist richtig?

To:

Dear Mr O'Shaughnessy

Thank you for your order which we **1.** received / replied a week ago. We are sorry to

2. say / inform you that Mr Kawamura who is in **3.** charge / responsible of your

order fell ill shortly after his return from China. He is likely to be **4.** absent / gone

from work for some time. Please accept our sincerest **5.** excuses / apologies

for failing to confirm your order in due course. Once again thank you for your

6. understanding / comprehension . Your order will be processed immediately.

Yours sincerely

Hiroaki Fujiwara
(P. A. to Akio Matsuo)

COMPUTER UND COMPUTERAUSSTATTUNG

13 **Equipment.** Benennen Sie Zubehör und Teile des Notebooks.

1. ....

2. ....

3. ....

4. ....

5. ....

6. ....

7. ....

8. ....

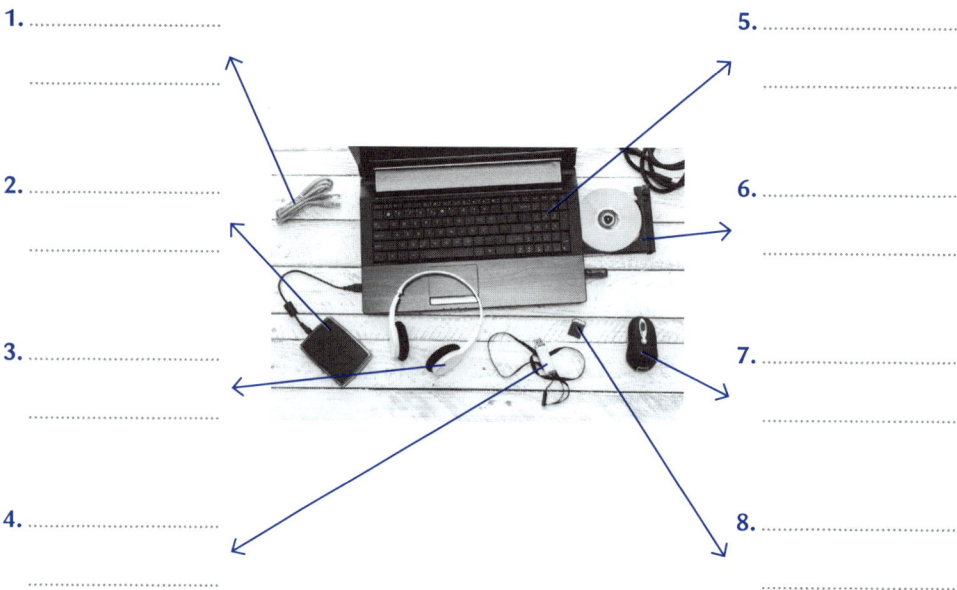

14 **Working with computers.** Was kann man mit einem Computer tun bzw. was kann passieren? Welche Übersetzung ist richtig?

1. hochfahren   a) ☐ to boot (up)   b) ☐ to boost   c) ☐ to brood

2. abstürzen   a) ☐ to crade up   b) ☐ to crash   c) ☐ to cast

3. neustarten   a) ☐ to reloot   b) ☐ to rebrew   c) ☐ to reboot

4. Daten speichern   a) ☐ to stone data   b) ☐ to store data   c) ☐ to stow data

5. ein-/ausloggen   a) ☐ to look up/down   b) ☐ to loft on/off   c) ☐ to log on/off

6. herunterfahren   a) ☐ to shut down   b) ☐ to shout down   c) ☐ to shoot down

7. einfrieren   a) ☐ to breeze   b) ☐ to freeze   c) ☐ to tease

15 **Working with files.** Was kann man mit einer Datei machen?
Übersetzen Sie die Verben.

1. to save

2. to download

3. to copy

4. to open

5. to delete ⟩ a file   eine Datei

6. to attach

7. to create

8. to upload

9. to close

....

....

....

....

....

....

....

....

....

16 **Prepositions.** Setzen Sie eine Präposition ein.

Alain: Hi Greg, I'm calling because several files have been deleted **1.** ....

my computer. Somebody must have used it.

Greg: Are you sure somebody deleted them intentionally?

There may be a virus **2.** .... one of your programs.

Alain: I don't know. Could you come **3.** .... and have a look?

Greg: Did you store all important files **4.** .... an external hard drive?

Alain: Yes, I did.

Greg: Good. By the way, I found some interesting information **5.** .... the internet.

Do you have access **6.** .... a different computer or smartphone at the moment?

Alain: Yes, of course.

TERMINE VEREINBAREN

1 **Making an appointment.** Enträtseln Sie die durcheinandergeratenen Wörter.

Receptionist: Carlton & Co. My name is Caroline Stowe.

Caller: Hi, this is Mike Brenton from RT&R. I'm ringing on **1. fahebl** .... of my

boss Mr Douglas. He asked me to make an **2. tippamonten** .... with

Ms Carlton for tomorrow afternoon if possible.

Receptionist: Let me check her **3. irday** .... – Would 2 o'clock be okay?

Caller: Ah, no, he'll still be in a **4. ginteem** .... A little later maybe?

What about 4 o'clock?

Receptionist: 4 o'clock would be fine.

Caller: All right, Mr Douglas will be at Ms Carlton's

5. foifec .... tomorrow at 4 p.m. Bye.

Receptionist: Thanks for **6. lagclin** .... Good bye.

2 Verbs with „appointment". Welches Verb ist richtig?

1. einen Termin vereinbaren = to make / take an appointment

2. einen Termin einhalten = to have / keep to an appointment

3. einen Termin verschieben = to postpone / move an appointment

4. einen Termin absagen = to negate / cancel an appointment

5. einen Termin bekommen = to get / obtain an appointment

6. einen Termin bestätigen = to confirm / agree an appointment

7. einen Termin haben = to have / possess an appointment

8. einen Termin verpassen = to miss / pass an appointment

Ein *appointment* ist ein Geschäfts- oder Arzttermin. Ein Termin beim Zahnarzt beispielsweise heißt *dentist's appointment*. Ein *date* hingegen ist entweder ein Rendezvous oder das englische Wort für „Datum":

to have a date with sb.	mit jmdm. eine Verabredung haben
to go out on a date	mit jmdm. ausgehen
the date on the invoice is ...	das Datum auf der Rechnung ist ...

3 Dates. Welche Übersetzung passt zu welcher Phrase?

1. ☐ today's date   a) der vereinbarte Tag / Termin

2. ☐ the agreed date   b) sich für einen Tag / Termin entscheiden

3. ☐ to fix a date   c) das heutige Datum

4. ☐ to decide on a date   d) zu einem späteren Zeitpunkt

5. ☐ at a later date   e) einen Termin festsetzen

6. ☐ delivery date   f) Mindesthaltbarkeitsdatum

7. ☐ sell-by date   g) Lieferdatum

4 Availability. Setzen Sie die passenden Begriffe in die Lücken ein.

see   free   suit   available   possible   convenient   make

1. When are you .... ?

2. Does Friday morning .... you?

3. Sorry, I can't .... it on Friday.

4. Would it be .... to arrange a meeting next week?

5. I'd like to make an appointment to .... Doctor Jones.

6. Would next Tuesday be .... ?

7. Will he be .... tomorrow morning?

TERMINE VERSCHIEBEN UND ABSAGEN

5 **Postponing an appointment.** Übersetzen Sie die Phrasen der Nachricht auf dem Anrufbeantworter.

Please leave a message after the tone.

"Hello, this is Fred Joyner. **1.** leidtun .... I have to

2. verschieben .... my appointment with you tomorrow morning.

I **3.** nicht schaffen .... it because I have an urgent appointment

with my bank. I mean I **4.** nicht einrichten können .... 9 o'clock –

I would **5.** frei haben .... in the afternoon, though. So, if you're

6. abkömmlich .... in the afternoon, say at 3 o'clock, please give me

a ring or write a short message. Thanks for your **7.** Verständnis ....

and sorry about the inconvenience. Goodbye."

6 **Types of meetings.** Welche Definition passt zu welchem Begriff?

1. ☐ follow-up   **a)** a large meeting of people with the same profession

2. ☐ conference   **b)** a friendly and informal meeting

3. ☐ video conference   **c)** a meeting between political leaders of several countries

4. ☐ convention   **d)** a large formal business meeting

5. ☐ get-together   **e)** a second meeting that follows a first one

6. ☐ summit   **f)** a meeting with people at different locations

Ein erster Termin oder ein erstes Treffen heißt *first* oder *initial appointment* bzw. *meeting*; alle weiteren sind *follow-up appointments* oder *follow-up meetings*. Im Britischen sagt man oft auch *to book an appoint-ment*, im Amerikanischen eher *to schedule an appointment*.

7 Terms with appointment and meeting. Finden Sie die englischen Übersetzungen der folgenden Wörter im Gitternetz.

O	P	U	W	D	A	F	F	M	N	L	U	O	E	D
D	E	F	O	R	E	S	C	H	E	D	U	L	E	E
C	A	R	L	O	F	F	A	T	T	E	N	D	X	F
D	B	E	D	E	A	D	L	I	N	E	E	D	A	I
Y	T	R	I	L	I	O	K	O	P	I	K	O	I	N
H	R	C	A	L	L	O	F	F	S	T	E	S	R	I
R	J	A	R	R	A	N	G	E	C	Y	E	S	E	S
A	E	C	Y	D	A	W	H	U	L	X	P	E	P	H

1. neu vereinbaren
2. teilnehmen
3. Abgabetermin
4. absagen (2 Wörter)
5. vereinbaren
6. Terminkalender
7. einhalten
8. beenden

8 Cancelling and apologizing. Übersetzen Sie die Sätze.

1. Ich muss den Termin mit Ihnen absagen.

....

2. Ich kann den Termin um 14 Uhr nicht einhalten.

....

3. Es tut mir leid, dass ich unseren Termin verpasst habe.

....

4. Ich hatte einen dringenden Termin bei meinem Anwalt.

....

5. Ich würde gern einen neuen Termin vereinbaren.

....

GESCHÄFTSBRIEFE

1 **A business letter.** Benennen Sie die Teile des Geschäftsbriefes.

salutation   signature block   addressee   reference   body (of the letter)
closing sentence(s)   letter head   closing salutation   date

Outdoor Fashion
Altdorfer Str. 25a
80990 München

1. ....

Ropa S.L.
C/ Tirant lo Blanc, 3
08034 Barcelona
Spain

2. ....

1 March 2018

3. ....

Dear Sir or Madam

4. ....

Enquiry about hiking sandals

5. ....

We saw your advertisement in the latest edition of the magazine *Senderismo* and would be interested in learning more about the hiking sandals you advertised. We are a small outdoor equipment store based in Munich and currently looking for new products.
We would be grateful if you could send us your latest catalogue and price list. We would also like to know if you offer discounts for large orders.

6. ....
....

We look forward to hearing from you soon.
(And sorry for not writing in Catalan.)

7. ....

Yours sincerely

8. ....

Emma Traunstein

Emma Traunstein

(General Manager)

9. ....

Auch wenn zwischen einer geschäftlichen E-Mail und einem Geschäftsbrief formal kein großer Unterschied sein sollte, ist ein Brief in der Regel noch etwas förmlicher.

2 **Types of letters.** Welches Wort passt zu welcher Übersetzung?

1. ☐ circular letter
2. ☐ quote/quotation
3. ☐ business letter
4. ☐ covering letter
5. ☐ reminder
6. ☐ letter of intent

a) Geschäftsbrief
b) Mahnung
c) Kostenvoranschlag
d) Rundschreiben
e) Absichtserklärung
f) Begleitschreiben

3 **Requests.** Jede Zeile enthält einen Tippfehler. Finden Sie ihn.

1. Could you please foreward us ... ?

2. We would be greatful if you could ... .

3. We would be much oblidged if you could ... .

4. I would apreciate it if you could ... .

5. I would be delignted if you could ... .

4 **Prepositions with "request".** Wählen Sie eine Präposition.

1. As / About requested, we are enclosing an update of our price list.

2. Further details will be provided on / over request.

3. The invoice was sent upon / by request of the head of department.

4. They have sent us an urgent request onto / for more information.

5 Saying thank you. Welcher Anfang passt zu welchem Satzende?

1. ☐ Thank you for your   a) advance for your efforts.

2. ☐ Thanks for doing   b) your understanding.

3. ☐ Thank you in   c) business with us.

4. ☐ Thank you for   d) attention to our enquiry.

5. ☐ Thank you   e) to our request.

6. ☐ Thank you for reacting   f) for your letter of 18 October.

6 As ... . Setzen Sie ein.

as per your   as you will see from   as stated

1. .... in our terms of business, we give a 10 % discount for repeat orders.

2. .... the enclosed brochure, we have lowered our prices.

3. The statement was issued .... request.

7 Friendly endings. Vervollständigen Sie die fehlenden Begriffe.

1. We wish to t _ _ _ _ _ y _ _ for your interest in our product.

2. We l _ _ _ f _ _ _ _ _ _ _ _ to serving you again.

3. We t _ _ _ _ _ that we will resume our business shortly.

4. We shall always be p _ _ _ _ _ _ _ to be of assistance.

5. We are c _ _ _ _ _ _ _ that you will be completely satisfied.

6. We would be delighted to r _ _ _ _ _ _ _ an order from you.

7. We are certain that our product will m _ _ _ all your requirements.

8. We will m _ _ _ every e _ _ _ _ _ _ to carry out future orders to your satisfaction.

8 With pleasure. Fügen Sie die Begriffe und Phrasen ein.

is with pleasure   take pleasure in   are pleased to   please let us know

1. We .... inform you that we dispatched your consignment yesterday.

2. It .... that we confirm the following offer.

3. .... if you have any queries.

4. We .... sending you the enclosed information pack.

9 Apologies and regrets. Welches Variante ist richtig?

1. We apologize for / about / on any inconvenience you may have had.

2. We offer our sincerest apologies as / on / for the delay.

3. We are sorry that / about / for the consignment did not arrive in time.

4. We are sorry for / of / on sending a faulty part.

5. We are sorry to have / have been / be enclosed the wrong documents.

6. We regret for / that / to our service fell short of your expectations.

10 Discounts. Setzen Sie die passenden Begriffe zusammen.

introductory   (cash)   loyalty   wholesale   import   volume/bulk/quantity

1. Skonto ....

2. Mengenrabatt ....

3. Einführungsrabatt ....

4. Großhandelsrabatt ....   discount

5. Stammkundenrabatt ....

6. Importrabatt ....

RECHNUNGEN

11 An invoice. Übersetzen Sie die Begriffe.

INVOICE

Invoice no.:   1. ....

Customer no.: 2. ....

Tax no.:   3. ....

Date: 4. ....

Service / Product / Description	Net price	VAT	Price
	5.		

6. ....   Subtotal:

7. ....   VAT:

8. ....   Total:

12 Payment phrases. Entscheiden Sie, welches Verb richtig ist.

1. Payments should be remitted / admitted within two weeks after receipt of invoice.

2. Please do / make all payments by bank transfer.

3. The travel agency allows / accepts all major credit cards.

4. It's advisable to settle / pay your account at the end of each month.

5. If you overdraw / overdrag your account you will have to pay overdraft interest.

13 Numbers & dates. Schreiben Sie die Zahlen und Daten aus.

1. 19 April 2018 ....

2. September 8, 2010 (*Am*) ....

3. ¥10,800.00 ....

4. 300,000,000 ....

5. 0.66 ....

6. 5.5 % ....

> Dezimalzahlen und Preisangaben schreibt man im Englischen mit einem Punkt statt einem Komma wie im Deutschen, z. B. 3.5 % oder £ 20.00. Ziffern über Tausend erhalten häufig ein Komma, um sie lesbarer zu machen, z. B. 255,000 oder € 12,500.00. Davon ausgenommen sind Jahreszahlen.

14 Payment terms. Setzen Sie eine Präposition ein.

1. bar zahlen   = to pay .... cash

2. mit der Kreditkarte zahlen   = to pay .... credit card

3. nach Erhalt der Rechnung bezahlen = to pay .... receipt of invoice

4. bei Lieferung zahlen   = to pay .... delivery

5. im Voraus zahlen   = to pay .... advance

15 Banking. Übersetzen Sie die Begriffe.

1. She opened her first `account` .... when she was thirteen.

2. The `account holder` .... was her father, though.

3. I set up a `direct debit` .... to pay the monthly rent.

4. Tenants usually pay regular bills by `standing order` ....

BESCHWERDEN UND MAHNUNGEN

16 A complaint. Entwirren Sie die Begriffe und fügen Sie sie in die E-Mail ein.

To:

Dear Sir or Madam

I would like to complain about the **1. seplsam** .... I received from you

yesterday. In our last email communication of 17 May, you **2. adeger** .... to

send me two samples free of charge. Instead you sent me half a **3. dezon** ....

items and **4. edecnlos** .... an invoice to be paid within a

5. frightont .... I am going to **6. rutren** .... four of the samples

and would like you to cancel the invoice. Thanks for your understanding.

Best regards

Beschwerden müssen deutlich die Ursache benennen, die für die Verstimmung gesorgt hat, und auf vorhergehende Absprachen, Vereinbarungen oder Bestellungen Bezug nehmen. Vorschläge zur Lösung des Problems sind ebenso ratsam sowie versöhnliche Worte, falls man weiterhin mit derselben Firma Geschäfte machen möchte.

17 Phrases. Welches Wort ist richtig?

1. I would like you to have a look into the matter / business .

2. There seems to have been a mistake / fault .

3. We would appreciate it if you could recruit / rectify the mistake you made.

4. We are very dissatisfied / unsatisfied with the service you provided.

5. I trust you will reinforce / reimburse me for the expenses incurred.

6. You seem to have calculated / charged the wrong item.

18 A reminder. Fügen Sie die Begriffe in die Mahnung ein.

oversights   overdue   disregard   submitted   outstanding

Invoice date: 12 June 2018
Invoice number: 45/590098

Dear Sir or Madam   16 July 2018

This letter is to formally remind you that the following invoice is now 14 days

1. .... We understand that **2.** .... sometimes happen

but would appreciate immediate payment of the **3.** .... amount. If you

have already **4.** .... payment, please **5.** ....

this letter and accept our apologies for any inconvenience this may have caused.

Yours sincerely

19 Types of information. Welcher Begriff passt zu welcher Übersetzung?

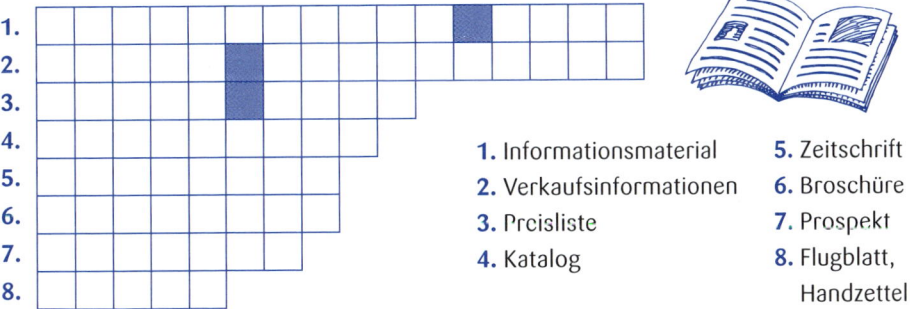

1. Informationsmaterial   5. Zeitschrift
2. Verkaufsinformationen   6. Broschüre
3. Preisliste   7. Prospekt
4. Katalog   8. Flugblatt,
                                Handzettel

Ein *flyer* ist ein einzelnes Blatt Papier mit Werbeinformationen,
das entweder zum Mitnehmen ausliegt oder auf der Straße verteilt wird;
ein *leaflet* ist ein gedrucktes und häufig gefaltetes Informationsblatt.

Im Büro

1 At the desk. Benennen Sie die Gegenstände.

1. ....

4. ....

5. ....

2. ....

6. ....

7. ....

3. ....

8. ....

2 On the desk. Welche Übersetzung gehört zu welchem Begriff?

1. ☐ hole punch   a) Radiergummi

2. ☐ scissors   b) Klebestift

3. ☐ rubber (*Am* eraser)   c) Reißzwecke

4. ☐ adhesive tape   d) Lineal

5. ☐ glue stick   e) Locher

6. ☐ ruler   f) Bleistiftspitzer

7. ☐ drawing pin (*Am* thumbtack)   g) Schere

8. ☐ pencil sharpener   h) Klebefilm

Auch Briten und Amerikaner verwenden gern den Markennamen für die Bezeichnung eines Alltagsgegenstandes. So, wie wir den durchsichtigen Klebestreifen als Tesafilm bezeichnen, nennt man ihn in Großbritannien *Sellotape* und in den USA *Scotch tape*. Australier sagen übrigens *sticky tape*.

3 More office equipment. Übersetzen Sie die Bürogegenstände.

1. Kaffeebecher
2. Pflanze
3. Kopierer
4. Drucker
5. Faxmaschine
6. Kaffeemaschine
7. Aktenschrank
8. Papierkorb

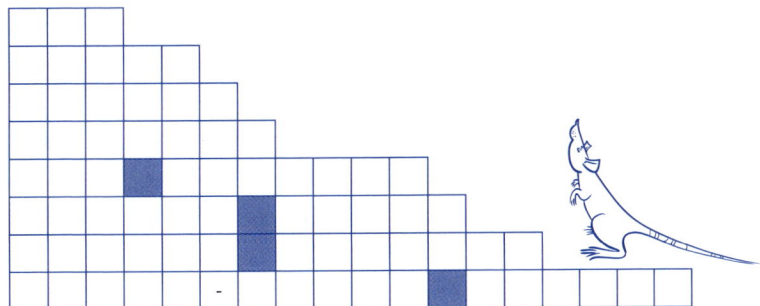

4 Office talk. Setzen Sie die Verben in der passenden Zeitform ein.

to order   to print out   to file   to run out of   to buy   to empty
to inform   to turn on

1. We've almost .... copying paper.

2. We also need .... a new ink cartridge for the laser printer.

3. Have you .... the stationery order?

4. Has anyone .... the boss about the change of plans?

5. Did you .... the invoices alphabetically?

6. Can someone .... the air-conditioning, please?

7. It's about time somebody .... the shredder again.

8. And who's turn is it .... some more coffee?

5 And how do you like your coffee? Übersetzen Sie die Begriffe und Phrasen.

Jane: I need three **1.** Tassen Kaffee .... in the morning to wake up.

Ron: I never drink coffee with **2.** Milch und Zucker .... – I like it black.

Mary: Be careful you don't **3.** verschütten .... coffee on the keyboard.

Pam: There are some **4.** Kaffeeflecken .... on your blouse.

Pete: Shall I **5.** machen .... some more coffee?

Don: Don't **6.** eingießen .... the coffee before I return from the bathroom.

Sue: This coffee is way too **7.** stark .... for me.

Lou: I guess I have to drink some **8.** entkoffeinierter Kaffee

.... for a change – I feel nervous all day.

6 More office talk. Welches Verb passt eher?

1. Has anyone taken care of / accepted the customer's request?

2. You need to address / label all new folders.

3. How long do you need to bet on / type up the handwritten minutes?

4. Listen to / Hear to the answering machine – there's a message for you.

5. I still have to corrective / proofread the invitations.

6. Have you arranged / arrangated a meeting with the sales representatives?

7 Word snake. Finden Sie acht Begriffe aus dem Büroalltag.

codacodeinmeetingceylondecolleaguesenvioiusagendasmenbrackageminutesbreakachewh
iteboardoutcallousconferenceroomcoagulateycanteenalmondsswivelchairoutrageouiengo

8 Postal service – products. Welcher Begriff ist richtig?

1. Brief   a) ☐ letter   b) ☐ envelope   c) ☐ brief

2. Eilbrief   a) ☐ hurried letter   b) ☐ express letter   c) ☐ urgent letter

3. Einschreiben   a) ☐ registered letter   b) ☐ regretted letter   c) ☐ on-written letter

4. Briefmarke   a) ☐ letter mark   b) ☐ stamp   c) ☐ brief mark

5. Paket   a) ☐ package   b) ☐ pack   c) ☐ packet

6. Päckchen   a) ☐ carton   b) ☐ small parcel   c) ☐ packaging

Die Begriffe *parcel* und *package* sind im Britischen identisch; im Amerikanischen wird *parcel* eher selten verwendet. Als *pack* oder *packet* bezeichnet man eine kleine Verpackung aus Papier, wie sie für Zigaretten (*pack of cigarettes*) verwendet wird, und *packaging* ist die Verpackung. Ein *carton* ist entweder eine Verpackung aus Pappkarton, z. B. *egg carton*, oder ein Tetrapack, wie in *milk carton* oder *carton of carrot juice*. – Porto heißt übrigens *postage*.

9 Postal service – phrases. Übersetzen Sie.

1. Hast du den Brief an Herrn Anthony schon aufgegeben?

....

2. Ist die Post schon dagewesen?

....

3. Ich werde den Brief morgen in die Post geben.

....

4. Es ist besser, den Brief als Einschreiben zu verschicken.

....

Tagesroutine

10 Employment. Finden Sie die richtige Übersetzung.

1. ☐ Vollzeitbeschäftigung   **a)** to work part-time

2. ☐ halbtags arbeiten   **b)** nine-to-five job

3. ☐ Gleitzeit   **c)** to work from home

4. ☐ Job mit geregelter Arbeitszeit   **d)** night shift

5. ☐ Nachtschicht   **e)** full-time job

6. ☐ von Zuhause arbeiten   **f)** flex(i)time

11 Prepositions. Setzen Sie die passende Präposition ein.

1. Betty sits behind her desk and works .... her computer all day.

2. Sandy writes, sends and receives quite a lot .... emails.

3. Minnie works mainly .... spreadsheets, charts and statistics.

4. Mr Stockton spends a lot of time .... departmental meetings.

5. Greg is usually .... the phone dealing with customer complaints.

12 Getting to work. Setzen Sie die Begriffe an passender Stelle ein.

commutes   walking distance   rush-hour traffic   company car   on the train

1. Mary-Lou spends over 50 minutes .... every morning.

2. Monica also .... to work by train – she hates driving.

3. Paddy lives within .... from his workplace.

4. The managing director has a ....

5. I prefer taking the bicycle to driving the car through ....

13 **Money matters.** Entscheiden Sie, welcher Begriff richtig ist.

1. I forgot to stop at the .... this morning to get some cash.

   a) ☐ cashier   b) ☐ cashpoint   c) ☐ cash register

2. Can we stop at the bank? I need to .... some money.

   a) ☐ take out   b) ☐ pull out   c) ☐ draw out

3. Every morning I go to the bank to .... the sales of the previous day.

   a) ☐ pay on   b) ☐ pay back   c) ☐ pay in

4. I make all payments by credit card or online by ....

   a) ☐ bank transfer   b) ☐ bank account   c) ☐ bank clerk

5. Is it still possible to ....?

   a) ☐ lose cheques   b) ☐ solve cheques   c) ☐ cash cheques

Im Geschäftsenglisch verwendet man auch die Verben *to withdraw* für das Abheben von Geld bzw. *to deposit* für das Einzahlen. – Der Geldautomat, der in Großbritannien *cashpoint* oder *cash machine* heißt, wird in den USA *ATM (automatic/automated teller machine)* genannt.

14 **Your job.** Beantworten Sie die folgenden Fragen auf Englisch.

1. What exactly do you do every day?

....

2. What do you enjoy most about your job?

....

3. How many hours a week do you work?

....

AUSZUBILDENDE UND PRAKTIKANTEN

15 Trainees. Setzen Sie eine Form *to train, training* oder *trainee* ein.

1. Kevin is looking forward to being .... as an office clerk.

2. I prefer on-the-job .... to theoretical courses at school.

3. Oscar is currently .... to be an accountant.

4. I started as a management .... three years ago.

5. Paula will be sent to Canada next year for further ....

6. Mr Russell is responsible for .... our people to be extra careful.

7. All our workers are regularly .... in new skills.

8. It's hard these day to find properly .... staff.

16 Apprentices. Setzen Sie eine passende Phrase ein.

for an apprenticeship   as an apprentice electrician   finding apprentices
    take on apprentices   was apprenticed to   a three-year apprenticeship

1. I served .... as a machine operator.

2. I've been working .... for two years.

3. She .... a small bakery in a nearby village.

4. Is it difficult to find people applying .... in plumbing?

5. Not all local factories .... anymore.

6. Some trades have problems ....

Ein weiblicher oder männlicher Praktikant heißt *intern* (nicht zu verwechseln mit *internee*, was Gefangener bedeutet); ein allgemeines Praktikum nennt man *internship*. Als Teil eines Unterrichts oder Studiums sowie als Maßnahme für Arbeitslose nennt man Praktikanten in Großbritannien auch *students/people on placement*.

ARBEITEN VON ZUHAUSE

17 Working from home. Welcher Begriff ist richtig?

Caller: Can I speak to Mr Thompson, please? This is Pete Marton.

PA: I'm sorry, but Mr Thompson is not **1.** in / on today. It's Friday, and he's working from **2.** home / house .

Caller: Oh, I didn't know that. Do you **3.** happen / have to have a number on which I can **4.** reach / react him. It's kind of urgent.

PA: Sure. It's 255-9589, but frankly it might be better to write an email. I know for sure that with this lovely weather his home **5.** bureau / office is his garden.

Caller: Thanks for **6.** talking / telling me. Good bye.

PA: Good bye, Mr Marton.

18 Home office. Finden Sie zwölf Fehler in den Fragen und Antworten.

Q: So, you've stared working from home. What's the difference between working from home and working in an offence?

A: First of all, I'm a lot many relaxed. I don't have to get dressed in the morning. I don't even have to get up at all, if I don't felt like it ..., well as least not as early as during the rest of the week. I can drink as much tea as I like while working and can even have a snake sitting next to my laptop. Nobody is complained when I decide to take half an hour of to read the newspaper or pop round to the shot to get something to eat.

Q: What is the minimum requirement for working from home in perms of equipment?

A: It almost goes without saying that I need fast interest – a good broadband connection is a basic requirement for my kind of word. But other than that ..., I have all the programs I need on my laptop. So I feel pretty independence.

SITZUNGEN

1 Types of meetings. Entwirren und übersetzen Sie die Sitzungstypen.

1. siscri meeting   ....

2. cymergene meeting   ....

3. arbod meeting   ....

4. cialesp meeting   ....

5. fasft meeting   ....

6. mitcomtee meeting   ....

> Eine ordentliche Jahreshauptversammlung wird meist *annual general meeting* genannt. Sitzungen können öffentlich (*public/open*) oder auch privat (*private/closed*) sein. Ein normales Geschäftstreffen heißt *business meeting*.

2 Verbs with "meeting". Welches Verb ist kein Synonym für das blau geschriebene?

1. to **arrange** a meeting

  a) ☐ to organize   b) ☐ to open   c) ☐ to convene   d) ☐ to set up

2. to **participate in** a meeting

  a) ☐ to depart in   b) ☐ to attend   c) ☐ to be present at   d) ☐ to be in

3. to **preside over** a meeting

  a) ☐ to conduct   b) ☐ to chair   c) ☐ to guest   d) ☐ to host

4. to **conclude** a meeting

  a) ☐ to finish   b) ☐ to close   c) ☐ to end   d) ☐ to detain

5. to **postpone** a meeting

  a) ☐ to put off   b) ☐ to delay   c) ☐ to cancel   d) ☐ to suspend

3 Collocations. Setzen Sie eines der folgenden Verben in der richtigen Form ein.

take (2x)   made   reach   hold (2x)   solve   raise

I told them that I was thinking about **1.** .... a crisis meeting. It shouldn't take too

long to **2.** .... the problem, I thought. Carl was going to **3.** .... the

minutes. During the meeting, they all **4.** .... good questions and **5.** ....

interesting points, but I still had my doubts. I suggested **6.** .... a vote by a show

of hands. But we weren't able to **7.** .... a decision; so I said I was afraid we would

have to **8.** .... another meeting the following week.

4 What's on the agenda? Bringen Sie die Silben in die richtige Reihenfolge.

1. We regularly hold ingstormbrain sionses .... to think
up new ideas.

2. The ingbrief .... was unnecessarily long and superfluous.

3. The gresspro portre .... was presented by the review committee.

4. The only item on the agenda was the getbud .... for the coming year.

5 Results of a meeting. Welche Verbform ist richtig?

Let me briefly tell you the results of our crisis meeting this morning:

– Gary was instructed to write / formulate a detailed report about the incidents

– Martin is supposed to take hold of / take care of the paperwork with the insurance

– The motion (*Antrag*) to install a new security system was carried / worn unanimously

– We were instructed how to deal about / deal with similar incidents in the future

– Carol was asked to take / write the minutes

DISKUTIEREN

6 Types of discussions. Welcher Begriff passt zu welcher Definition?

negotiations   argument   debate   talks   discussion

1. long and intense discussion about a subject ....

2. a heated debate between people with different opinions ....

3. conversation between people about different aspects of a subject ....

4. official discussions between two or more groups ....

5. formal discussions between governments ....

7 Agreeing and disagreeing. Setzen Sie das passende Wort ein.

what   more   up   with   to was

1. I very much agree .... you on this aspect.

2. I couldn't agree .... with what you've just proposed.

3. We agreed .... have another meeting the following week.

4. It .... agreed that we all should try harder.

5. I disagree completely with .... you've just said.

6. I agreed .... to a certain point, but now I'm afraid I have to contradict.

8 Questions. Welche Phrasen gehören zusammen?

1. ☐ How do you   a) thoughts on all of this?

2. ☐ Do you all agree   b) say anything about this?

3. ☐ What do   c) feel about the matter?

4. ☐ Do you want to   d) you mean?

5. ☐ What are your   e) with what Mary has just told you?

Wird keine Einigung erzielt, hört man im Englischen oft *We agreed to disagree*, womit man zum Ausdruck bringt, dass man zwar uneins war, aber nicht unversöhnlich auseinandergegangen ist.

9 Disagreement. Wie heißt das markierte Verb in der deutschen Grundform?

1. Two of the members simply refused to give their consent. ....

2. We differed widely on what to do next. ....

3. Half the members dissented from the suggestions made. ....

4. Carol took issue with her boss's decision. ....

5. The group was completely divided on the issue. ....

6. Some clients reneged on the agreement. ....

10 Phrasal verbs. Setzen Sie die richtigen Präpositionen ein.

It took us hours to work **1.** .... a compromise. It's always difficult to come **2.** ....

a decision. We didn't even agree **3.** .... the agenda. We decided to vote **4.** ....

the resolution. Carl finally came **5.** .... a new idea. But we never really

arrived **6.** .... a conclusion.

11 Discussion phrases. Ordnen Sie die typischen Einleitungsphrasen.

1. I be wrong might, but ... .

2. to me it seems that ... .

3. opinion in my... ....

4. I'm as far concerned as ... .

5. ask you if me well, ...

PRÄSENTATIONEN

12 Charts et al. Benennen Sie die Darstellungsformen.

bar chart   pie chart   organization chart   line chart   table   area chart

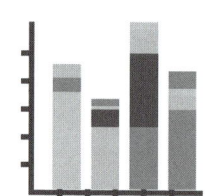   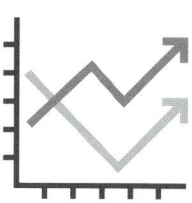

1. ....   2. ....   3. ....

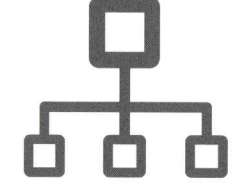   

	Mon	Tues	Wed
5			
4			
3			
2			
1			

4. ....   5. ....   6. ....

13 Describing charts. Welches Satzende passt zu welchem Anfang?

1. ☐ The chart shows that sales   a) as follows: ...

2. ☐ As you can see from the chart,   b) went up in the second quarter.

3. ☐ The third quarter results are   c) for overall sales last year.

4. ☐ Let's go over the figures   d) sales were excellent in the first half of the year.

14 Column chart. Benennen Sie die Teile der Graphik.

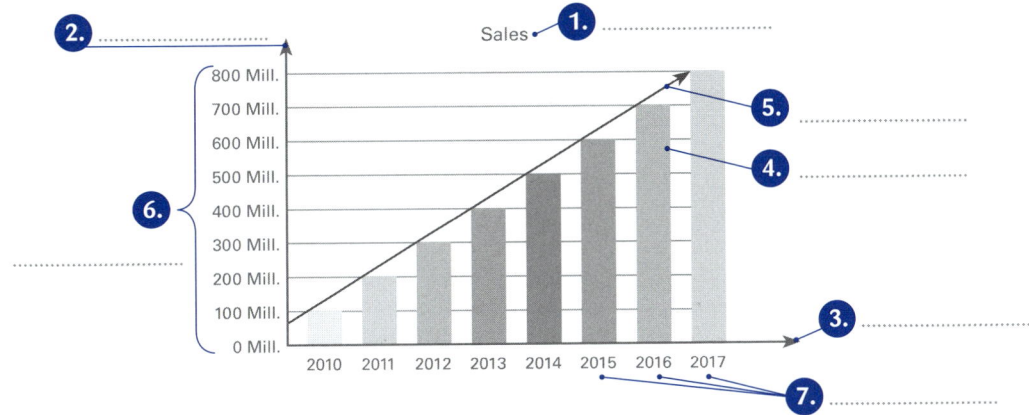

15 Attention, please! Setzen Sie das passende Verb ein.

turn   have   pay   give   received

1. Can I .... your attention, please?

2. We need to .... more attention to what our competitors are doing.

3. Since the relaunch we have .... a lot of attention in the media.

4. Let me .... your attention to the consumer price index.

5. Would you please .... a bit more attention.

16 Cause and effect. Wählen Sie die richtige Präposition.

1. The increase was caused by / from the weakness of our competitors.

2. The decrease was a result on / of a very bad start after the summer holidays.

3. The recovery was brought of / about by the launch of our new product in early autumn.

4. This gave rise to / for a confident outlook into next year.

5. Last year's performance resulted on / in a 20 % increase in annual revenues.

GÄSTE UNTERHALTEN

1 **Small talk topics.** Erraten Sie fünf typische Smalltalkthemen.

1. ☐ _ M _ _ Y

2. _ ☐ R _

3. S_ ☐ R _

4. _ _ L _ ☐ _ Y _

Lösung: _ _ _ _ _

> Das Wort *sport* steht im Britischen wie im Deutschen im Singular und im Amerikanischen im Plural: *I do a lot of sport(s).* Den Plural verwenden Briten für zusammengesetzte Begriffe wie *sports club* oder *sports event* sowie als Übersetzung für „Sportarten".

2 **Questions.** Übersetzen Sie die Fragen.

1. Interessieren Sie sich für moderne Kunst?

....

2. Trinken Sie lieber Kaffee oder Tee?

....

3. Hatten Sie einen guten Flug?

....

4. Schauen Sie gern Sport?

....

5. Was für Essen mögen Sie?

....

6. Sind Sie schon mal hier gewesen?

....

7. Wie gefällt Ihnen unsere Stadt?

....

3 The weather - odd one out. Welches Adjektiv passt nicht in die Reihe?

1. good	sultry	lovely	nice
2. humid	perfect	glorious	beautiful
3. fine	sunny	muggy	dry
4. awful	dreadful	terrible	fair
5. appalling	mild	nasty	rotten
6. windy	stormy	hot	heavy
7. wet	damp	rainy	bright

weather

Nicht überall ist das Wetter Thema Nummer eins. In Ländern, in denen das ganze Jahr über gleiche Wetterbedingungen herrschen, spielt das Wetter in der täglichen Kommunikation keine Rolle. In Singapur beispielsweise unterhält man sich viel lieber über das Essen.

4 Rain, rain, rain. Entscheiden Sie sich für die richtige Form?

1. I think it is / was going to rain any minute.

2. I've never saw / seen so much rain in my entire life.

3. The forecast says there'll be even more / much rain tonight.

4. Does it rain / rains a lot in your country?

5 Weather idioms. Welche Definition passt zu welchem Ausdruck?

1. ☐ to feel under the weather   a) to make sth. more complicated than it is

2. ☐ to weather sth.   b) in all types of weather

3. ☐ to make heavy weather of sth.   c) to come through a difficult situation

4. ☐ in all weathers   d) to not feel well

6 Films. Fügen Sie die Begriffe in die Lücken ein.

scenery   love-hate relationship   latest film   affordable
prices   capturing   big screen   weather conditions

Host: Have you seen the **1.** .... by Dora Myers?

Guest: Oh, yes, I saw it just last week.

Host: What did you think about it?

Guest: I thought it was superb. The **2.** .... is breathtaking.

Myers did a great job in **3.** .... the atmosphere of this

strained relationship between father and son.

Host: You're right – this complicated **4.** .... between the two

is brilliantly reflected by the **5.** .... up north.

Guest: So, is going to the cinema still **6.** .... in your country?

Host: Not really anymore. It used to be a lot cheaper, so I actually don't go very often.

Guest: Same here. The **7.** .... have gone up quite a bit lately.

Host: I know it's a shame. But seeing these fantastic landscape images

on a **8.** .... was just worth it.

7 Film talk. Fügen Sie die Begriffe in die jeweilige Spalte ein.

interesting   documentary   awful   adventure   love   thriller   bad   drama
can't stand   entertaining   hate   comedy   enjoy   mainstream   adore

1. type of film				
2. liking/disliking				
3. opinion				

GESELLIGES BEISAMMENSEIN

8 An invitation. Setzen Sie passende Präpositionen ein.

1. Do you have plans .... this evening?

2. Our department would like to invite you .... dinner tonight.

3. Do you like Scottish food? It's not .... bad .... it sounds.

4. There's a famous pub .... the corner that offers a wide variety of local specialities,

mainly fish and sea food. You do like fish, don't you?

5. No, there's no need to dress .... It's very informal.

6. I hope you don't mind walking. It's really not far .... here.

7. Yes, you'd better take an umbrella. The weather is unpredictable all year ....

In britischen Pubs bestellt man Essen und Getränke am Tresen. Die Mahlzeit wird dann in der Regel aber am Tisch serviert. Die Person hinter dem Tresen heißt *barman* oder *barmaid* und erwartet übrigens kein Trinkgeld (*tip*). Man kann sie jedoch einladen, in dem man *And one for you* sagt.

9 Beer. Erraten Sie die Biersorten und finden Sie ein Getränk auf Apfelbasis.

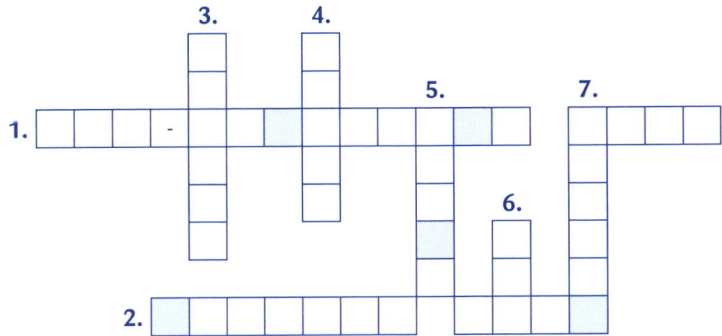

1. beer without alcohol
2. beer from a tap
3. beer mixed with lemonade
4. very dark strong beer
5. light-coloured beer
6. typically British beer
7. brown strong beer

Lösung: An alcoholic drink made from apples: _ _ _ _ _ _

10 **Pub talk.** Entscheiden Sie, welche Form richtig ist.

Maria: Could you speak **1.** up / higher a bit? I can't hear you –

the television is so **2.** loudly / loud .

John: Sorry, would you like to go **3.** somewhere / anywhere else?

Maria: No, it's okay, I don't mind **4.** watching / to watch football, but I **5.** hard / hardly

get a word of what they're saying.

John: Oh, you should be here on a quiz night. If you think this is loud, just wait ...

Maria: Quiz night? Sounds interesting, but I **6.** expect / await the questions to be very

British, about British history and **7.** entertainment / entertaining and stuff.

John: Yeah, sometimes, but it really depends on the pub. **8.** Let's / Let me ask if there's

a quiz night this week.

11 **In a pub.** Übersetzen Sie.

1. Können Sie mir etwas empfehlen?

....

2. Die nächste Runde geht auf mich.

....

3. Bekommt man hier etwas zu essen?

....

Wasser ist mit oder ohne Kohlensäure erhältlich (*with gas* oder *without gas*).
Nicht-alkoholische, kohlensäurehaltige Limonaden jeglicher Art nennt man
soft drinks (oder speziell *lemonade* oder *soda water; Am soda*):
Could you get me a bottle of lemonade from the bar, please?

12 **Socializing.** Entwirren Sie das Wort und beantworten Sie die Fragen auf Englisch.

1. How often do you **azocilsie** .... with your colleagues after work?

....

2. Do you **alecebert** .... the birthdays of your colleagues in the office?

....

3. Have you ever had a close **altonishreip** .... with a colleague?

....

13 **Expressing one's thanks.** Welches Satzende passt zu welchem Anfang?

1. ☐ Thank you very much **a)** invite me to your birthday party.

2. ☐ It's been very kind of you to **b)** to be part of this special event.

3. ☐ I feel very pleased **c)** for this wonderful evening.

14 **National holidays.** Wann und in welchen Ländern werden diese Feiertage begangen?

1. Human Rights Day **a)** ....

2. Spring Bank Holiday **b)** ....

3. St Patrick's Day **c)** ....

4. Anzac Day **d)** ....

Der wichtigste Feiertag in den USA ist *Thanksgiving*. Er wird immer am vierten Donnerstag im November gefeiert. Der Freitag danach, den man auch *Black Friday* nennt, ist für viele arbeitsfrei: Das ist das einzige richtig lange Wochenende im Jahr. In Kanada wird *Thanksgiving* übrigens am zweiten Montag im Oktober begangen.

EIN HOTELZIMMER BUCHEN, UMBUCHEN UND STORNIEREN

1 Reservation. Schreiben Sie die fehlenden Begriffe in die Lücken.

To:

Dear Sir or Madam

On behalf of my boss, Daniela Maibach, I would like to **1.** r _ _ _ _ _ _ _ an ensuite

double room with **2.** b _ _ _ _ _ _ _ _ _ between 10 and 16 October. Ms. Maibach

intends to visit the Vancouver Design Festival. Since I assume that your hotel is

3. n _ _ - s _ _ _ _ _ _ _, it would be nice if the room had a **4.** b _ _ _ _ _ _ _

or small terrace. Ms. Maibach will be arriving quite late on a flight from Düsseldorf with

a stopover in Toronto and certainly be **5.** j _ _ - _ _ _ _ _ _ _, so she would

appreciate it if you could **6.** p_ _ _ _ her _ _ _ from the airport or provide another

kind of **7.** s _ _ _ _ _ _ s _ _ _ _ _ _ _ to your hotel. Looking forward to

8. h _ _ _ _ _ _ from you soon.

Best regards

Alina Grossmann (P.A. to Ms. Maibach)

2 Accommodation. Ordnen Sie die Namen richtig zu.

motel   5-star hotel   B&B

1. .... **2.** .... **3.** ....

3 **Confirmation.** Setzen Sie die Begriffe in die Lücken ein.

smoking lounge   breakfast buffet   tax   flight information   airport   second floor

Dear Ms. Grossmann

We've reserved an ensuite double room for Ms. Maibach from 10 and 16 October

incl. **1.** .... You're right in assuming that our hotel is non-smoking,

but the rooms have neither balconies nor terraces. Instead there's a comfortable

2. .... on the **3.** .... open 24 hours to all our guests.

The price of the room is CAD 185.00 per night, **4.** .... included.

Please tell us Ms. Maibach's **5.** .... as soon as possible – we're happy

to arrange for her to be picked up from the **6.** ....

We're looking forward to welcoming Ms. Maibach in Vancouver.

Best wishes
Anthony Jong

4 **Change of plans.** Welche ist die richtige Schreibweise?

Dear Mr. Jong

Thank you for your prompt **1.** reply / rely . We need to make a slight **2.** charge / change ,

though. I've just found out that the **3.** fight / flight from Düsseldorf to Toronto is already

4. foolly / fully booked. So Ms. Maibaum will be **5.** arriving / arrival one day later,

that's 11 October, on flight no. AC 119 from Toronto, **6.** scheduled / sheduled arrival

at 18.14h. I hope this doesn't cause you too much inconvenience.

Thanks for your understanding.

Alina Grossmann

5 Cancellation. Übersetzen Sie die blauen Passagen.

Anthony: Hotel Vancouver, this is Anthony Jong speaking.

Alina: Hi, this is Alina Grossman calling from Germany.

Anthony: Hello Ms Grossmann. How can I help?

Alina: Mr Jong, I'm very sorry to tell you that **1. I need to cancel the reservation** for my boss, Ms Maibach. **2. She was involved in a car accident** last night and is now unable to start off with the journey.

Anthony: I'm very sorry to hear that. **3. Let me check my computer.** – Ah, yes, she'd reserved a double room from tomorrow until the 16th.

Alina: Yes, and I would like to cancel the entire stay.

Anthony: All right. But you do know that a cancellation fee of 20% will apply **4. at this short notice.**

Alina: Yes, I know, but I'm sure my boss will choose your hotel again next year. **5. She's totally devastated** about not being able to go. Is there anything you can do?

Anthony: Ms Grossmann, I'll make a note about that. Your boss will have to pay the cancellation fee right now, but she will also be able **6. to offset the fee against the hotel bill** next year if she happens to come.

Alina: Thank you very much, Mr Jong, we'll keep in touch. Good bye.

Anthony: Good bye, Ms Grossmann.

1. ....

2. ....

3. ....

4. ....

5. ....

6. ....

HOTELANLAGEN UND RAUMAUSSTATTUNG

6 Facilities. Ordnen Sie die Hoteleinrichtungen und -anlagen richtig zu.

parking area   fitness room   ensuite bathroom   lounge   sauna   lobby/reception

1. ....   2. ....   3. ....

4. ....   5. ....   6. ....

7 Furnishings. Ordnen Sie die Begriffe den Beschreibungen zu.

bedside table (*Am* nightstand)   queen-size bed   wardrobe   walk-in closet
(Venetian) blind (*Am* shades)   lampshade   armchair

1. a large cupboard for hanging clothes   ....

2. a window cover that can be pulled up and down   ....

3. a small table beside the bed   ....

4. a cover for a lamp   ....

5. a bed that is smaller than a king-size bed   ....

6. a comfortable chair with arm rests   ....

7. a closet that is large enough to walk into   ....

8 The bed. Welches Bettzubehör verbirgt sich hinter welchem Begriff?

1. ☐ linen   a) Tagesdecke

2. ☐ bedspread   b) (Woll)decke

3. ☒*f* pillow   c) Bettlaken

4. ☐ duvet (*Am* comforter)   d) Steppdecke

5. ☐ sheet   e) Bettwäsche

6. ☐ quilt   f) Kopfkissen

7. ☐ blanket   g) Federbett

9 Complaints. Setzen Sie den passenden Begriff ein.

toilet   towels   sheets   TV   air-conditioning

1. The .... doesn't work.

2. The .... seems to be blocked.

3. The .... have not been changed.

4. There are no .... in the bathroom.

5. I can't turn on the ....

10 Getting connected. Übersetzen Sie die Begriffe.

1. Do you have WLAN .... in all rooms?

2. Do I need a Passwort ...., Pin ....

   or Code .... to log in?

3. Is there a computer with free Zugang .... to the Internet I could use?

4. Where can I make Auslandsgespräche .... ?

AM EMPFANG

11 **At reception.** Enträtseln Sie die durcheinandergeratenen Begriffe.

Guest: Good evening. I have a **1. aserveirton** ....

                    The name is Borchardt, Martin Borchardt.

Receptionist: Could I see some form of **2. aitnifictodein** ...., please?

Guest: Sure. Here's my **3. asopprst** .... Would that be okay?

Receptionist: Yes, of course, you've reserved a double room without breakfast

                    for 3 nights. Is that correct?

Guest: Correct.

Receptionist: Mr Borchardt, this is your **4. akcryed** .... Your room is

                    on the third floor; the number is 312. The **5. ateveorl** ....

                    is over there. Do you have any other wishes?

Guest: Yes, do you have a **6. arb** .... or lounge where I

                    can get something to drink?

Receptionist: Yes, it's down this **7. aseil** .... on the right hand side.

Guest: Thank you.

Receptionist: You're welcome. Enjoy your **8. atsy** ....

12 **Questions.** Welcher Begriff ist richtig?

1. What time do I have to check out / check up ?

2. Where can I leave my packings / luggage until my plane leaves?

3. Do you have a safe where I could leave my valuables / worthables ?

4. Do you take this debit card / EC-card ?

5. Is there a laundry and platting service / ironing service ?

REISEN MIT DER BAHN

1 At the ticket counter. Setzen Sie die Begriffe ein.

platform   underground fare   single ticket   tube ticket   first-class   train

Traveller: I'd like to have a **1.** .... **2.** ....
to Edinburgh for tomorrow morning.

Employee: Certainly.

Traveller: What time does the **3.** .... arrive?

Employee: It leaves from King's Cross at 9.00 a.m. and arrives in Edinburgh Waverley
Station at 1.20 p.m.

Traveller: And what **4.** .... does it leave from?

Employee: It leaves from platform 3.

Traveller: Is the **5.** .... included?

Employee: No.

Traveller: So I need to buy an extra **6.** .... from my hotel to the station?

Employee: Yes, that's right. Here's your ticket.

Traveller: Thank you very much.

Employee: You're welcome.

2 On a US train. Ordnen Sie die Wagentypen zu.

1. ☐ dining car   a) Panoramawagen

2. ☐ sleeping car   b) Speisewagen

3. ☐ panorama car   c) Salonwagen

4. ☐ lounge car   d) Schlafwagen

EIN AUTO MIETEN

3 Hiring a car. Welche Schreibweise ist richtig?

1. I have a reservation for a medium-sized / middle-sized car.

2. I have an international driving license / driving licence .

3. It says "everything is included" on my reservation sheet / sheat .

4. No, I don't need any extra insurence / insurance .

5. I'd like to return the car with a full tank / tanck .

4 Types of cars. Ordnen sie die Fahrzeugtypen zu.

estate car, (*Am*) station wagon   saloon car, (*Am*) sedan   convertible

sports car   four-wheel drive/SUV   hatchback

1. .... **2.** .... **3.** ....

4. .... **5.** .... **6.** ....

An vielen Tankstellen der Welt muss man die Oktanzahl kennen, um das Richtige zu tanken. Häufig gibt es *regular* (87), *premium* (93) bzw. *supreme* (93) oder auch *super* (93) und *plus* (98) und natürlich *diesel*. In den USA wird in *gallons* zu je 3,79 Litern verkauft; Öl erhält man in *quarts* zu je 0,95 Litern.

AUF DEM RICHTIGEN WEG

5 Asking for directions. Übersetzen Sie die Begriffe.

Drive up to the Ampel **1.** t _ _ _ _ _ _ _ l _ _ _ _ _ _. Take the right Spur

2. _ _ _ _ _, turn right and then take the second street on the left. After a few hundred

yards you'll come to a Kreisverkehr **3.** r _ _ _ _ _ _ _ _ _ _ _ where you have

to take the third exit. Don't take the Umgehungsstraße **4.** r _ _ _ _ r _ _ _ _ _ –

that would be the second exit. Stay on that road for two miles and you'll see a Tankstelle

5. p_ _ _ _ _ _ s _ _ _ _ _ _ _ on your left. Turn left right after the petrol station

and take the first on your left. It's a Einbahnstraße **6.** o _ _ _ - w _ _ _ s _ _ _ _ _ _

and it will lead up to a Kreuzung **7.** c _ _ _ _ _ _ _ _ _ _ _ where you turn right and

after a hundred yards you'll see the post office on your right hand side.

6 Not far from here. Bringen Sie die Sätze in die richtige Reihenfolge.

1. there   a   with   Is   casualty   department   a   in   vicinity   the   hospital?

....

2. local   know   you   a   pub   around   with   specialities   here   Do?

....

3. nearest   Where   the   is   garage?   tyre   got   flat.   I've   a

....

7 Odd one out. Welcher Begriff passt nicht in die Reihe?

1. turnpike	toll bridge	toll road	tunnel
2. beltway	ring road	overpass	bypass
3. crash	pile-up	rear-end collision	traffic jam

IM RESTAURANT

8 Ordering. Setzen Sie die passende Phrase ein.

for dessert   rare   ready to order   side order   as a starter   main course

Waiter: Are you **1.** ....?

Pam: Could I have a tomato salad **2.** ....?

Mike: I'll have the pepper steak for the **3.** .... No starter for me.

Waiter: How do you like your steak: **4.** ...., medium or well-done?

Mike: Medium, please.

Pam: For me the lamb cutlets with a **5.** .... of chips and a small salad, please.

Mike: Is there anything you would recommend **6.** ....?

> In vielen Restaurants im Ausland ist es nicht üblich, sich einfach an einen Tisch zu setzen. Man bekommt von einem Kellner entweder einen Tisch zugewiesen oder wird gefragt, wo man gern sitzen möchte.

9 Complications. Setzen Sie ein passendes Wort ein.

The hotel restaurant offered a full menu à la carte, but when I looked at the Speisekarte

.... I felt lost – it was all in French! So I decided to have a look at the

Weinkarte .... first and ask for a menu in English. Somehow, the waitress

brought a Kinderkarte ...., but anyway, I found something that looked

ansprechend .... to me. After waiting for 30 minutes for my Essen

..........................., I decided to sich beschweren .... to the waiter. He was

very sorry, and my food arrived within minutes. However, instead of the Beilagensalat

.... that I had ordered, I got mashed potatoes, which I hate.

10 Types of restaurants. Tragen Sie die Übersetzung ein und finden Sie einen weiteren Restauranttyp.

1. Schnellimbiss _ _ _ _ _ - _ _ _ _ ☐ restaurant

2. Fischrestaurant _ ☐ _ _ _ restaurant

3. romantisches Restaurant _ _ _ _ _ ☐ _ _ _ _ restaurant

4. Selbstbedienungsrestaurant _ _ _ _ _ - _ ☐ _ _ _ _ _ _ _ restaurant

5. Vier-Sterne-Restaurant _ _ _ _ _ - _ _ _ _ ☐ restaurant

Lösung: family ☐ ☐ ☐ ☐ ☐

🍃 *It's tea time!* 🍃

Als *diner* oder auch *family diner* bezeichnet man Speiserestaurants (in den USA), die in ihrer Qualität zwischen Schnellgaststätten und hochwertigen Restaurants liegen, häufig preiswert und familienfreundlich sind und qualitativ gutes Essen anbieten.

11 Adjectives. Ordnen Sie die Adjektive den passenden Begriffen zu.

posh   tasty   fixed-price   high-end (*Am*)   gourmet   delicious

nutritious   cocktail   dessert   three-course   organic   four-star

Restaurant	Food	Menu

Imbissbuden, in denen man ostasiatische oder indische Speisen zum Mitnehmen erhält, oder auch solche, die *hot dogs* oder *fish & chips* anbieten, nennt man in Großbritannien *takeaway* und in den USA *takeout*.

12 **Bills and tips.** Übersetzen Sie die Sätze.

1. Kann ich bitte die Rechnung haben?

....

2. Kann ich mit Kreditkarte zahlen?

....

3. Auf der Rechnung scheint ein Fehler zu sein.

....

4. Die Restaurantrechnung belief sich auf 65 Pfund ohne Trinkgeld.

....

5. Ich bat die Bedienung, mir die Rechnung zu bringen.

....

6. Wir ließen 15 Prozent Trinkgeld auf dem Tisch (liegen).

....

Sollen Rechnungen aus dem hoteleigenen Restaurant oder der Hotelbar auf die Gesamtrechnung des Hotelaufenthalts gesetzt werden, so sagt man umgangssprachlich: *Put it on my tab/bill, please.*

13 **Cab to the hotel.** Welche Version ist richtig?

1. Could you name / call me a taxi, please?

2. Where's the nearest / next taxi stand around here?

3. Please turn up / on the meter.

4. You can drop me off / out at the corner.

5. How much cost / is it to the Best Western on Cromwell Road?

6. Please pull over / out in front of the convenience store.

7. Keep the change / charge .

JOBANZEIGEN UND BEWERBUNGSSCHREIBEN

1 **A job advert.** Fügen Sie die Verben und Adjektive an der richtigen Stelle ein.

represent   existing   talented   leading   support   include

Market **1.** .... event agency

is looking for a **2.** .... event manager

to **3.** .... their team. Focus of the

position is to **4.** .... the agency

Event Manager	
Recruiter:	Medion Event Agency
Location:	Manchester
Salary:	£ 30,000 – £ 35,000
Hours:	full time

in the U.K. and Ireland via a combination of new business strategies and key account

management techniques. The role will **5.** .... strategic development

of **6.** .... events into new European locations.

2 **Your profile.** Welche Variante ist richtig?

You will have **1.** profound / pro-forma experience in event marketing, specifically

in **2.** large-scale / large-range events, and you also like working in a team. You will

be a **3.** hardly working / hard-working and **4.** ambitious / ambiguous professional

who is happy to do business over the phone and by email. You speak at least one

5. strange / foreign language fluently, will have to travel on occasion, conduct

6. face-to-face / head-to-head meetings, and attend events all over Europe.

Dank des technologischen Fortschritts sind Bewerbungen im Ausland heute nicht mehr kompliziert. Jobannoncen findet man ebenso online wie Informationen über alle bürokratischen Erfordernisse, die man für einen Arbeitsaufenthalt im Ausland erfüllen muss, wie Arbeits- und Aufenthaltserlaubnisse, Krankenversicherung und Steuerregelungen. Hilfreich ist es in jedem Fall, sich durch die Lektüre von Blogs oder Erfahrungsberichten vorzubereiten.

3 Curriculum vitae. Setzen Sie die Überschriften ein.

Professional Experience   Education   Objective   Personal Information   Skills   Interests

---

CURRICULUM VITAE

SABINE SABINSEN
Sabinenstr. 9, 50111 Cologne
++49 (0)221 123 4568
info@sabine.de

1. .... Intelligent and responsible event manager seeking position in an established event agency. Gained extensive experience from working in large event agencies in Germany and England.

2. ....
Date of birth	1 January 1985
Place of birth	Cologne, Germany
Nationality	German

3. ....
2004–2008   Media Academy, Cologne
(BA in Event Management)
1995–2004   Secondary School (Gymnasium),
Cologne (Abitur = A Levels)
1991–1995   Primary School

4. ....
2014–today   Dekanter Event & Catering GmbH, Munich
Full-time employment. Responsible for organizing and budgeting major events for prestigious clients.
2013–2014   The Castaway Ltd., Brighton
Worked part-time in a team and participated in all events.
Attended Cambridge course and passed CPE test.
2009–2013   Town-Ho Event Agency, Hamburg
Practical training with subsequent employment. Responsible for planning events and consulting clients. Developed incentives and marketing strategies.

5. ....
Languages	German (native speaker)
	English (C2 – CPE Cambridge Certificate)
	Spanish (B2)
Computer	MAC, Windows, Adobe programs

6. .... Tennis (club member), fashion, art, travelling

In einigen englischsprachigen Ländern ist es üblich, die persönlichen Daten auf Name, Adresse und Telefonnummer zu beschränken. Es wird also weder ein Foto beigefügt noch Lebensdaten oder Familienverhältnisse angegeben. In den USA nennt man den Lebenslauf übrigens *résumé*.

4 **Cover letter.** Setzen Sie die gegebenen Infinitive in der richtigen Form ein.

Dear Sir or Madam

I am interested in the position as event manager in your agency as **1.** to advertise

.... on your website. I am currently **2.** to employ ....

as an event manager in a large event agency in Munich, Germany. I believe that the skills

and experience I **3.** to gain .... at this position make me the ideal

candidate for the job you offer.

As event manager **4.** to work .... with companies and prestigious clients,

I have developed strong planning, organizational and marketing skills.

I have also gained considerable experience in **5.** to stage .... large events

and last but not least in convincing clients.

I am confident that my experience qualifies me for consideration. Please find **6.** to enclose

my CV. If you are interested, I can also **7.** to provide .... you with letters

of recommendation. I would enjoy the opportunity **8.** to discuss ....

my qualifications in more detail and look forward to hearing from you soon.

Sincerely yours

Sabine Sabinsen
Enclosure

5 Application phrases I. Entwirren Sie die Begriffe.

1. I would like to apply for the position savertedid .... in the *Guardian.*

2. I have some carapctil .... experience in the brewing trade.

3. I am used to working in a team and enjoy giwkron .... with people.

4. I etrinda .... as an internet editor at a local advertising agency.

5. I have just completed a six-month eplentcam .... at a logistics company.

6. I speak English and French fluently and have a working gnewdeolk ....
of Russian.

7. I would be able to start at short coniet .... and also be prepared
to move to Manchester.

8. I would welcome an tipyropunot .... to introduce myself at an interview.

6 Application phrases II. Übersetzen Sie ins Deutsche.

1. I saw your advertisement for the post of insurance broker on your homepage.

....

2. After completing the A levels, I trained as an office administrator.

....

3. Since 2014, I have been working for a leading marketing firm.

....

4. I would enjoy working for a British company.

....

5. I enclose my CV and a letter of recommendation.

....

VORSTELLUNGSGESPRÄCH

7 Interview questions. Welcher Satzanfang passt zu welchem Satzende?

1. ☐ What are your reasons   a) overtime and at weekends?

2. ☐ What exactly did you   b) for wanting to work in England?

3. ☐ What do you expect   c) your interests?

4. ☐ Are you ready to relocate   d) do in your training?

5. ☐ When would you be able to   e) as a starting salary?

6. ☐ Are you willing to work   f) lived abroad?

7. ☐ What are   g) and travel a lot?

8. ☐ Have you ever   h) start work?

8 Bad impression. Was macht bei einem Vorstellungsgespräch keinen guten Eindruck? Finden Sie die Begriffe und setzen Sie das Lösungswort zusammen.

1. L A C K   O F   C O _ ☐ I _ E _ C _

2. L A C K   O F   P _ E _ _ _ _ A _ _ _ ☐ N

3. L A C K   O F   ☐ _ R _ E R   P _ _ N _ _ _ _ G

4. L A C K   O F   E _ _ _ H ☐ ☐ _ A _ M

5. P O O R   G R _ ☐ _ _ A _

6. L A C K   ☐ F   I _ T E _ _ S T

7. L I M P   H _ ☐ D _ _ A _ ☐

8. L A C K   O F   C O _ R _ E S ☐

Lösung: _ _ _ _ _ _   on _ _ _ _ _ _ _

Grammatik

1 Simple or progressive? Setzen Sie das Verb in der konjugierten oder der ing-Form ein.

1. Sam usually to start .... work at 8 in the morning.

2. Maria is currently to work .... for a trendy fashion designer.

3. Abdul and Amy to answer .... dozens of phone calls every day.

4. Juan to love .... to travel abroad twice month.

5. Lin to write .... the minutes of yesterday's meeting at the moment.

6. George to think .... about how to reduce costs.

7. Candy to want .... to be a nurse after finishing her internship.

Mit dem *Present simple* drückt man regelmäßige Tätigkeiten und Tatsachen aus; das *Present progressive* wird für aktuelle und unvollendete Tätig-keiten in der Gegenwart verwendet. Verben, die einen mentalen Vorgang beschreiben, wie *to believe, to know, to remember* oder *to suppose* stehen nur selten, andere, wie *to need, to seem, to own* oder *to cost*, die gar keine Tätigkeit ausdrücken, stehen nie in der *Progressive form*.

2 Progressive or not? Welche Form ist richtig?

1. We need / are needing to make sure that we make a good impression.

2. The marketing manager tries / is trying to find a solution to the problem.

3. There seems / is seeming to be a mistake in the invoice.

4. The new advertising assistant does / is doing a good job.

5. As of September 1, all IT consultants get / are getting a pay rise.

6. The PA to Ms Matthisson expects / is expecting a baby.

7. Mr Dawson doesn't know / isn't knowing how to fix the photocopier.

8. We've run out of steam. I think / am thinking we need to relaunch the campaign.

3 Static and cognitive verbs. Setzen Sie die Verben in der richtigen Form ein.

to afford   to use   to not finish   to show   to cost   to suppose

1. Don't put the calculator away. I .... it.

2. Tickets to the farmer's market .... £10 per person and per day.

3. I think Sue .... some Chinese visitors around.

4. The meeting .... until 5.30.

5. Prices for electric cars will drop soon, I ....

4 Sensory verbs. Übersetzen Sie.

1. Ich hasse es, den ganzen Tag Rechnungen schreiben zu müssen.

....

2. Die Insolvenz seines Hauptkonkurrenten berührt ihn überhaupt nicht.

....

3. Die ganze Angelegenheit riecht nach Korruption.

....

4. Ich mag es wirklich nicht, wenn der CFO die Firma in den Himmel lobt.

....

5. Ich hoffte, dass mein Chef Ende des Jahres in Rente gehen würde.

....

> Verben der Sinneswahrnehmung wie *to smell, to taste* oder *to touch* stehen
> nur dann in der *Progressive form*, wenn sie tatsächlich eine *Tätigkeit*
> ausdrücken. Das gilt auch für die Verben des Liebens und Hassens:
> *to like, to dislike, to love* und *to hate*.

5 Past tense or Present perfect. Welche Form ist richtig?

1. Prices .... on average by 20 percent this year.

    a) ☐ dropped   b) ☐ were dropping   c) ☐ have dropped   d) ☐ have been dropped

2. They hastily .... a press conference yesterday morning.

    a) ☐ arranged   b) ☐ were arranging   c) ☐ have arranged   d) ☐ have been arranging

3. We .... in a meeting when the news of the accident broke.

    a) ☐ sat   b) ☐ were sitting   c) ☐ have sat   d) ☐ have been sitting

4. The company has told over 100 employees that they .... redundant.

    a) ☐ made   b) ☐ were made   c) ☐ have made   d) ☐ have been made

> Das *Past tense* beschreibt vergangene Zustände und Tätigkeiten, die keinen Bezug zur Gegenwart haben. Das *Present perfect* (have/has + 3. Form) dagegen stellt einen Zusammenhang zwischen der Vergangenheit und der Gegenwart her, indem es Zustände und Tätigkeiten beschreibt, die noch anhalten oder vor Kurzem beendet wurden, aber noch Auswirkungen auf die Gegenwart haben.

6 A crisis meeting. Setzen Sie die Verben in der richtigen Zeitform ein.

We **1.** to have .... a crisis meeting the other day. It **2.** to be .... my

first crisis meeting since I **3.** to join .... the company two years ago, and it will

certainly be my last. Honestly, I **4.** to never see .... anything more unstructured

than our head of department. We all **5.** to sit .... there listening to his blabbering

for hours, and nobody **6.** to dare .... to interrupt him. I **7.** to talk ....

to him twice since then, but he doesn't seem to understand, and, of course, we

8. to deal .... with our issues yet. I think I'm going to leave this sinking ship.

7 **Right or wrong?** Welcher Satz ist richtig. Kreuzen Sie an.

1. a) ☐ The company has been based in Bristol since the merger.

b) ☐ The company was based in Bristol since the merger.

2. a) ☐ We closed our subsidiary in Singapore shortly before the crisis.

b) ☐ We have closed our subsidiary in Singapore shortly before the crisis.

3. a) ☐ After the bankruptcy of Fontson & Co, I started working for S&A again.

b) ☐ After the bankruptcy of Fontson & Co, I have started working for S&A again.

4. a) ☐ We had our head office in Perth since 1998.

b) ☐ We've had our head office in Perth since 1998.

5. a) ☐ Two years after the restructuring our MD left the company.

b) ☐ Two years after the restructuring our MD has left the company.

6. a) ☐ The company found a lot of new investment opportunities in recent years.

b) ☐ The company has found a lot of new investment opportunities in recent years.

8 **Since and for.** Setzen Sie *since* oder *for* ein.

1. We've been quite successful on the market .... more than 20 years.

2. We have attracted several new customers .... we moved our office to Glasgow.

3. Prices have risen by 4 percent as a result of the fall in the pound .... the Brexit vote.

4. Inflation has remained steady .... the past six months.

5. Consumer spending is growing at the fastest rate .... 2012.

6. They've been talking .... over three hours.

7. I've met the CEO twice .... I started working here.

8. Our relationship has improved .... I talked to him.

9 The substitute. Entscheiden Sie sich für die richtige Form.

Pat: **1.** Did you see / Have you seen Betty?

Sid: Yes, eh ..., well no, she **2.** called in / has called in sick this morning.

Pat: Oh, sorry to hear that. Who **3.** is sitting in / sits in for her?

Sid: You mean, who **4.** will be in charge of / is being in charge of taking the minutes this afternoon?

Pat: Ah, yes.

Sid: I guess that'll be your job. You **5.** are / have been the official substitute secretary.

Pat: Well, all right.

Sid: Don't you remember? In our last meeting, we **6.** were choosing / chose you as Betty's replacement in case of her absence.

10 Present perfect simple or progressive? Setzen Sie das Verb in eine der beiden Formen.

1. Carl to write .... emails for over three hours.

2. Sue to talk .... to 12 customers so far – now she needs a break.

3. Tony to work .... in his father's company for two years now.

4. Mr Clarke to just return .... from a business trip to Sydney.

5. Mary to always want .... to see Niagara Falls.

6. Ms Brown to be .... Mr Clarke's PA since she joined the company.

Die *Simple form* verwendet man für unmittelbar zuvor abgeschlossene oder noch anhaltende Zustände und Tätigkeiten, deren Ergebnis aktuell noch relevant ist; die *Progressive form* findet bei Tätigkeiten Verwendung, die in der Vergangenheit anfingen und in der Gegenwart noch anhalten.

11 Questions. Ordnen Sie die Wörter zu sinnvollen Fragen und setzen Sie dabei das kursiv gedruckte Verb in die richtige Zeitform.

1. firm   the   established?   When   *to be*

....

2. the   going   did   How   bank   bankrupt?   *to avoid*

....

3. year?   a   the   in   company   rise   this   Has   sales   *to achieve*

....

4. people   today?   many   How   *to miss*

....

5. have   of   the   do   Why   half   trainees   money?   *to borrow*

....

12 Present perfect and Past perfect. Welche Form ist richtig?

1. When we got back home, we saw that someone had broken / has broken into

the garden shed while we were on holiday.

2. How long had he had / has he had this car? – I think for about two years now.

3. There you are! I have been waiting / had been waiting for over an hour.

4. When we arrived at the stadium, the game has already begun / had already begun .

Die Formen des *Past perfect* (had + 3. Form) verwendet man für Handlungen in der Vorvergangenheit, d. h. zwei vergangene Handlungen werden
in Beziehung gesetzt, wobei die eine vor der anderen geschehen ist.

13 Will and going-to future. Setzen Sie die richtige Form ein.

will do   am going to   will be   are going to   is going to

1. I'm sure our new client .... very satisfied with your work.

2. Did you answer that email? – Oh, I completely forgot, I .... it right away.

3. I've made up my mind – I .... apply for a new job.

4. I can already feel it – prices .... fall soon.

5. According to the news, the company .... to set up a new subsidiary in Spain.

Das G*oing-to future* wird vor allem für Pläne und Absichten verwendet sowie dann, wenn die unmittelbare Zukunft bereits zu erahnen ist. Das W*ill-future* hingegen steht bei spontanen Antworten, bei allgemeinen Vorhersagen für die fernere Zukunft sowie für zukünftige Fakten und Zustände.

14 Other future forms. Setzen Sie das Verb in eine der Zukunftsformen.

1. The whole department to go .... to the pub on Friday evening.

2. What are your plans for this afternoon? – I to see .... my dentist at 2.

3. Tomorrow morning I to sit .... on a plane to Dubai.

4. At 4.30 this afternoon I to still work ....

5. The train from Birmingham airport to arrive .... at 12.55h.

Die Formen des *Present simple* verwendet man für Zeitpläne bei zukünftigen Ereignissen, z. B. Fahrpläne oder Abfahrtszeiten; die Formen des *Present progressive* stehen für feststehende Termine in der Zukunft. Das *Future progressive* beschreibt temporäre Tätigkeiten zu einem Zeitpunkt in der Zukunft.

15 **Phrases for future events.** Setzen Sie die für Zukünftiges häufig verwendeten Wendungen ein.

was on the verge of   is certain to   was about to   is to visit   is due   are to be

1. I .... leave the office when the phone rang.

2. The new sales tax .... cause annoyance among small business owners.

3. The old warehouse .... collapsing when we had it demolished.

4. The consignment .... to arrive tomorrow morning.

5. The invoices .... sent off by Friday afternoon.

6. The new CEO .... our subsidiary in Japan next week.

16 **Future in the past.** Welche Form ist richtig?

1. I .... call the new client this morning, but I completely forgot.

  a) ☐ am going to   b) ☐ was going to   c) ☐ were going to

2. We .... open the meeting when the fire alarm went off.

  a) ☐ were about to   b) ☐ are about to   c) ☐ had been about to

3. Last year the company .... filing for bankruptcy.

  a) ☐ is on the edge of   b) ☐ were on the edge of   c) ☐ was on the edge of

4. She told me she .... finish the report this afternoon.

  a) ☐ would   b) ☐ will   c) ☐ wants

Wird die Zukunft von der Vergangenheit aus gesehen, verwendet man meist die Vergangenheitsform des *Going-to future*: *was/were going to*. Auch die oben vorgestellten Wendungen *was about to* oder *was on the verge/edge/brink of* können Zukünftiges in der Vergangenheit ausdrücken. In der indirekten Rede wird die Zukunft mit *would* gebildet, wenn das Verb des Sagens in der Vergangenheit steht.

1 Adjectives ending in -ing and -ed. Übersetzen Sie die Adjektive.

The presentation this afternoon was pretty langweilig **1.** ....

The speaker was verwirrend **2.** .... and his talk had no structure.

I was not the only one who was gelangweilt **3.** .... The whole

department thought there was nothing really interessant **4.** ....

about what he said. The department head was begeistert **5.** .... ,

though, when he heard the good sales figures. After listening for more than two hours

we were all quite erschöpft **6.** .... and happy to go home.

> Englische Adjektive sind in Singular und Plural sowie bei männlichen
> und weiblichen Substantiven unveränderlich. Sie haben folgende Endungen:
> *-y, -ly, -ic, -ical, -ous, -ful, -less, -able, -ible, -ish.* Ferner können Partizipien
> auf *-ing* und *-ed* ebenfalls als Adjektive verwendet werden.

2 Adjectives. Wandeln Sie – soweit möglich – die Substantive in Adjektive um.

	-y	-less	-ous	-ful
1. cloud	....	....	....	....
2. wealth	....	....	....	....
3. end	....	....	....	....
4. joy	....	....	....	....
5. colour	....	....	....	....
6. help	....	....	....	....
7. luck	....	....	....	....
8. danger	....	....	....	....

3 Adjective or Adverb? Entscheiden Sie, welche Form richtig ist.

1. The CEO remained calm / calmly when she heard about the accusations.

2. Our sales manager turned red / redly in the face because he was embarrassed.

3. When the committee questioned the vice president, she appeared quite

nervous / nervously .

4. The marketing manager grew pale / palely when his former PA entered the room.

5. The committee has evidence that will prove them guilty / gultily .

6. In the office no one is angry / angrily about the way things have developed.

7. The new secretary only said that our coffee tasted awful / awfully .

> Nach den Verben *to appear, to become,*
> *to get, to go, to grow, to prove, to remain,*
> *to seem, to stay* und *to turn* sowie den Verben
> der Sinneswahrnehmung, wie
> *to look, smell, to taste* oder *to touch,*
> steht immer ein Adjektiv, wenn das Verb
> *keine* Aktivität ausdrückt.

4 Adverbs of frequency. Kreuzen Sie die möglichen Position(en) des Adverbs an.

1. usually   a) ☐, Ms Jackson b) ☐ starts work at 9 in the morning.

2. never   a) ☐ Mary-Lou b) ☐ talks to anyone about her new book.

3. sometimes   a) ☐ Martin b) ☐ feels like he should look for a new job.

4. always   a) ☐ Mr Dawson b) ☐ locks the windows when he leaves the office.

5. occasionally   a) ☐, Meggie b) ☐ has to travel abroad.

5 Adjective or Adverb? Welche Form ist richtig? Kreuzen Sie an.

1. The project manager took the .... train to Edinburgh.

   a) ☐ direct   b) ☐ directed   c) ☐ directly

2. The Chinese delegation arrived at ....12 o'clock.

   a) ☐ exact   b) ☐ exactedly   c) ☐ exactly ✕

3. James had .... arrived at the agency when the phone rang.

   a) ☐ just   b) ☐ justing   c) ☐ justly

4. I have the impression they .... ever seem to work.

   a) ☐ hard   b) ☐ hardily   c) ☐ hardly

5. They whole department arrived .... to the party.

   a) ☐ late   b) ☐ lated   c) ☐ lately

6. Ms Clarkson was .... upset when she found out about the fraud.

   a) ☐ quite   b) ☐ quitedly   c) ☐ quitely

6 Adjective order. Welche Reihenfolge der Adjektive ist richtig?

1. Sue bought a leather brown nice .... briefcase.

2. Last night Herb wore a old business grey .... suit.

3. I talked to an English interesting young ....
   writer at the book fair.

4. The CV was in a plastic green dirty .... folder.

Mehr als drei Adjektive hintereinander vor einem Substantiv zu verwenden ist stilistisch unschön. Die gängige Reihenfolge ist folgende: *Urteil – Größe – Form – Alter – Farbe – Herkunft – Material – Verwendung – Substantiv.* Meist hat man jedoch bereits ein Gefühl für eine „gut klingende" Reihenfolge der Adjektive.

7 Comparisons. Füllen Sie die Tabelle mit den unregelmäßigen Steigerungsformen aus.

1.	good		
2.		worse	
3.			least
4.		elder	
5.	much		

Die Formen *elder* und *eldest* verwendet man nur für Personen; bei Dingen ist die Steigerung von *old* regelmäßig: *old, older, oldest.*

8 Ungradable adjectives. Übersetzen Sie die nicht-steigerbaren Adjektive.

1. enorm, immens   _ _ _ _ _ _ _ ☐ _

2. fantastisch, toll   _ _ ☐ _ _ _ _ _ _

3. schrecklich, furchtbar   _ _ _ _ ☐ _ _ _

Q

4. wundervoll, wunderbar   _ _ _ _ _ _ _ ☐ _

5. riesig, gewaltig   _ _ _ ☐

Lösung: ☐ ☐ ☐ q ☐ ☐

Nicht-steigerbare Adjektive wie *perfect* drücken etwas Absolutes aus. Sie können weder mit *most/more* noch mit *very* gesteigert werden. Interessanterweise ist aber das Adverb *absolutely* als Beschreibung zulässig und gebräuchlich. Ebenfalls nicht steigerbar sind Adjektive, bei denen eine Steigerung unsinnig ist, wie *dead* oder *married.*

9 Odd one out. Welches Wort ist *kein* Adverb?

1. ☐ lately   2. ☐ mostly   3. ☐ friendly   4. ☐ very   5. ☐ well

10 Negative prefixes. Setzen Sie eine passende negative Vorsilbe ein.

1. ....fortunately for the company, its main supplier had to file for bankruptcy.

2. I'm pretty much used to working ....regular hours.

3. He had never been able to explain his ....logical behaviour.

4. All staff waited ....patiently in front of the factory hall.

5. With all due respect, I ....agree completely with what you're saying.

6. Our line manager is very ....sensitive about our problems.

7. The union speaker said that the treatment of the strikers was ....fair.

8. All our rooms are ....-smoking.

11 Adjective or Adverb? Entscheiden Sie sich für die richtige Form.

1. The new trainee impresses by his friendly / friendlily manners.

2. The chauffeur wasn't driving too fast / fastly when the accident happened.

3. The report you sent me last week was real / really helpful.

4. It's important that we all get equal / equally pay for equal work.

5. What would you do if you were unfair / unfairly dismissed from work?

6. She told me that all rental cars were full / fully insured.

12 Less & few. Setzen Sie few, fewer, less oder least ein.

1. Our new copier uses .... energy than the old one.

2. .... people know how to fill in a tax form correctly.

3. HR has received no .... than 150 applications so far.

4. I didn't have the .... idea how to write a business report.

13 Sentence structure. Bringen Sie die Wörter in die richtige Reihenfolge.

1. manufactured   are   our   for   professional   tools   All   use   multi-purpose

....

2. are   goods   wooden   wrapped   and   Fragile   crates   shipped   in

....

3. not   consignment   The   was   last   against   handling   improper   insured

....

4. commissioned   international   very   forwarder   we   The   was   reliable   freight

....

5. wage   has   new   government   to   promised   increase   minimum   the   The

....

14 Comparisons. Übersetzen Sie die deutschen Wendungen.

1. Alistair earns genauso viel wie .... Tammy.

2. Fiona usually works schneller als .... Jonathan.

3. Martha is wesentlich erfahrener als .... Susan.

4. They have bei weitem nicht so viel .... turnover.

5. Our competitor's products are geringfügig billiger als .... ours.

6. Last year they worked kaum so effizient wie .... this year.

> Vergleiche erfolgen mit den Ausdrücken *as … as* und *Komparativ + than*.
> *As … as* kann mit Wörtern wie *hardly, just, almost, (not) nearly,*
> *nowhere near* oder *(not) quite* umschrieben werden – *Komparativ + than*
> mit *far, much, a lot, a bit* oder *slightly*.

1 **Truths and statements.** Setzen Sie die vorgegebenen Verben ein.

| take | stressed out | freezes | don't get | is | turn on | tend to be | try |

1. If you feel ...., you should .... a break and start again.

2. If your program ...., ... restarting the PC first.

3. If people .... enough sleep, they .... tired and nervous.

4. If the office .... hot and sticky, why don't you ....
the air-conditioning?

> Konditionalsätze haben meist zwei Teile: einen If-Satz, in dem eine Bedingung
> ausgedrückt wird, und einen Hauptsatz, der die Folge der Bedingung beschreibt.

2 **What if ...** Setzen Sie die Verben in die richtige Form.

1. When I `to drink` .... too much coffee,

I usually `to get` .... nervous.

2. If Cathy `to not return` .... from lunch soon,

you `to have` .... better `to give` .... her a call.

3. If Conrad `to buy` .... the tickets this morning,

we `to go` .... to the computer fair next week.

4. If it `to not rain` ...., we can `to have` .... lunch in the park.

5. If you `to have` .... any queries, `to not hesitate` .... to call me.

> Bei Konditionalsätzen der Gegenwart und Zukunft (Typ I) steht im Haupt-
> satz *will-future* (auch *Present simple* oder ein *Imperativ*) und im If-Satz
> *Present simple.* Je nach Aussage sind im If-Teil *Present progressive*
> und *Present perfect* ebenfalls möglich.

3 **A storage problem.** Entscheiden Sie sich für die richtige Variante.

Liv: You **1.** will be / would be on the safe side if you use an external hard drive.

Ivy: Yes, but if I **2.** store / stored every file

in the cloud, I won't have to worry about

an extra gadget which might break after a while.

Liv: That's true, but how can you be sure the cloud

3. doesn't / didn't create any problems in the future?

If I **4.** am / were you, I'd be careful and not rely on the cloud.

Ivy: I'll **5.** have / had to ask my boss first if he's willing to spend another £ 40 or so.

Liv: So? I just wouldn't take any chances if I **6.** have / had such delicate material.

Bei Konditionalsätzen, die einen eher unrealistischen Wunsch oder eine hypothetische Idee für die Gegenwart oder Zukunft ausdrücken (Typ II), steht im Hauptsatz *would + Infinitiv* und im If-Satz eine Form des *Past tense*.

4 Mix up. Setzen Sie die beiden Satzhälften zusammen.

1. ☐ If I worked in Canada, a) please get me some transparent film, too.

2. ☐ I'd soon be promoted, b) I would celebrate Thanksgiving in early October.

3. ☐ If I were allowed to retire soon, c) if your headache doesn't go away.

4. ☐ When you leave the office, d) I could move to southern Europe.

5. ☐ If you do the stationery order, e) make sure all the lights are turned out.

6. ☐ You should call in sick, f) you should complain to the management.

7. ☐ If you don't like our canteen, g) if I only could force myself to work harder.

5 Translation. Übersetzen Sie die Sätze.

1. If Tom isn't invited for a job interview, he'll apply somewhere else.

....

2. What would you do if you were to lose your job next month?

....

3. Would Patricia be willing to work overtime if required?

....

4. If our factory were to close down soon, we'd all get financial compensation.

....

> Die Konstruktion *were to* im If-Teil des Konditionalsatzes drückt eine eher unwahrscheinliche Situation in der Zukunft aus, die im Deutschen gern mit dem Verb *sollte* übersetzt wird.

6 Negative if-clauses. Verneinen Sie die Verbform.

1. I would love to go out with you if I to have to .... work tonight.

2. He was certainly in a meeting if he to be .... in his office.

3. If only the trade union leader to always talk .... for so long ...

4. Give me a ring if you to be .... able to open the program.

5. If Pam leaves the office in time, she to have .... any problems to catch the train.

> Im If-Teil des Satzes verneint man Hauptverben mit *don't/doesn't* oder *didn't* sowie Hilfsverben und to be-Formen mit *not*. Im Hauptsatz steht *won't* oder *wouldn't*.

7 Types. Zu welchem Typ gehört der Satz? Kreuzen Sie an.

1. Daniel will come home any minute if the bus is on time.

a) ☐ Typ I (Bedingung erfüllbar)   b) ☐ Typ II (Bedingung nur theoretisch erfüllbar)

2. Daniel would come home any minute if the bus was on time, but it never is.

a) ☐ Typ I   b) ☐ Typ II

3. If Daniel catches the 4 o'clock bus, he'll arrive at a quarter to six.

a) ☐ Typ I   b) ☐ Typ II

4. If Daniel caught the 4 o'clock bus, he'd arrive at a quarter to six.

a) ☐ Typ I   b) ☐ Typ II

5. It's 5.30. If Daniel has caught the 4 o'clock bus, he'll be home soon.

a) ☐ Typ I   b) ☐ Typ II

6. If Daniel's boss hasn't asked him to work late, he'll be sitting on the 4 o'clock bus now.

a) ☐ Typ I   b) ☐ Typ II

If you can dream it, you can do it!

8 Assumptions. Welche Form ist richtig?

1. Supposing that / Supposed that you've made the wrong decision –

what will you do then?

2. Providing that / Provided that you're fit and your knee doesn't hurt anymore,

you can fly to Toronto next week and attend the conference.

3. Giving that / Given that backing down is out of the question,

we need to brace ourselves for tough negotiations.

> Die Formulierungen *supposing (that), provided (that), given (that)* wie auch *on condition that, as long as* und *inasmuch as* verwendet man im formalen wie im schriftlichen Englisch gern als Ersatz für ein schlichtes *if*.

9 **Unless.** Welche Aussagen sind identisch? Markieren Sie mit richtig + oder falsch –.

1. a) ☐ Unless we invest at once, it will be too late.

  b) ☐ If we don't invest at once, it will be too late.

2. a) ☐ I won't know where to meet you at the fair, unless you send me a message.

  b) ☐ I won't know where to meet you at the fair, if you don't send me a message.

3. a) ☐ Don't call the systems administrator if your computer freezes again.

  b) ☐ Don't call the systems administrator unless your computer freezes again.

10 **Mistakes.** Finden Sie je einen grammatischen Fehler in den Sätzen.

1. Unless you want to do the same job until you retire, you would have to get off

  your backside and start writing applications.

2. I'll ask Jake about it, unless you will prefer me talk to the department head first.

3. The company can't afford to expand activities unless it merged with its main competitor.

4. Unless we established a subsidiary, we won't benefit from any tax deductions.

11 **Provided that.** Setzen Sie die beiden Phrasen an der richtigen Stelle ein.

provided that   **unless**

1. We're having a board meeting tomorrow .... the CEO is sick.

2. We're having a board meeting tomorrow .... the CEO is well again.

12 If only ... Welche Formen sind richtig? In einigen Fällen sind es zwei.

1. If only our agency .... afford more adverts in prestigious magazines.

   a) ☐ can   b) ☐ could   c) ☐ will   d) ☐ would

2. If only my husband .... spend so much money on suits and ties.

   a) ☐ don't   b) ☐ doesn't   c) ☐ didn't   d) ☐ won't

3. I'd love to travel the world, if only I .... more time and money.

   a) ☐ have   b) ☐ has   c) ☐ had   d) ☐ would have

4. If only you .... how hard I tried to get this job.

   a) ☐ know   b) ☐ knows   c) ☐ will know   d) ☐ knew

5. It took me three hours to get here. If only I .... taken the train.

   a) ☐ had   b) ☐ hadn't   c) ☐ have   d) ☐ don't have

6. If only it .... fake news – but unfortunately, the story was real.

   a) ☐ was   b) ☐ were   c) ☐ have been   d) ☐ had been

> Nach *if only* steht in der Regel *Past tense* für gegenwärtige Wünsche oder *Past perfect* für Wünsche, die in der Vergangenheit liegen. Nach *I wish* folgt *Past tense*, wenn man sich die Änderung eines Zustandes wünscht, und *would* oder *could*, wenn man sich eine *aktive* Änderung wünscht.

13 I wish ... Übersetzen Sie die deutschen Verben.

1. I wish I wüsste .... more about this program, I wouldn't have to call IT so often.

2. I wish I hätte .... more time to learn how to create websites.

3. I wish I wäre .... 20 years younger, I'd enroll in a computer course.

4. I wish I könnte fliegen .... to Rome – the weather there is much nicer.

5. I wish I würde verdienen .... twice as much – I could afford a new car.

6. I wish I hätte angerufen .... the client yesterday.

1 Indirect speech. Setzen Sie die Sätze in die indirekte Rede.

1. "The MD is in a meeting."   He said he .... in a meeting.

2. "Susan is having lunch."   He said she .... lunch.

3. "We can do it tomorrow."   He said we .... it tomorrow.

4. "They haven't placed an order yet."   He said they .... an order yet.

5. "He's been working in sales for ages."   He said he .... in sales for ages.

6. "Mary may work from home next year."   He said Mary .... from home next year.

> Steht das einleitende Verb der *indirekten Rede* in der Vergangenheit,
> z. B. *said* oder *told sb.*, so verschiebt sich die Verbform der direkten Rede
> um eine Zeitstufe in die Vergangenheit. Steht die direkte Rede im *Past tense*,
> kann sie unverändert bleiben oder ins *Past perfect* verschoben werden.
> Das *will* im *Future* wird zu *would*. – Steht das einleitende Verb der indirekten
> Rede in der Gegenwart, wird die Verbform nicht verändert.

2 Change of tenses after "He said …". In welche Zeitform ändert sich das Verb in der indirekten Rede?

1. Present simple   ⟶   ....

2. Present progressive   ⟶   ....

3. Past simple   ⟶   ....

4. Past progressive   ⟶   ....

5. Present perfect simple   ⟶   ....

6. Present perfect progressive   ⟶   ....

7. Future I (will)   ⟶   ....

8. Future II   ⟶   ....

3 Auxiliary verbs. Auch die Hilfsverben ändern sich – aber nicht alle! Wohin verschieben sich die Hilfsverben in der indirekten Rede?

1. can $\longrightarrow$ ....

2. shall $\longrightarrow$ ....

3. will $\longrightarrow$ ....

4. must $\longrightarrow$ ....

5. could $\longrightarrow$ ....

6. should $\longrightarrow$ ....

4 Translation. Setzen Sie die Sätze in die indirekte Rede.

1. "I closed my account because the bank had raised the charges."

She said ....

2. "We expect you to pay our invoice by the end of the month."

He said ....

3. "I'll sign the contract as soon as I get it."

Martha said ....

4. "I'm a constable and I'm sure I can't be made redundant."

Pete said ....

5 Say sth. and tell sb. Entscheiden Sie, welches Verb richtig ist.

1. She said / told she would finish work at 4 today.

2. Frank said / told me he didn't have any time this weekend.

3. The line manager said / told something I didn't understand.

4. Tell / Say her to hand in the report by Friday 6 p.m.

5. Please don't say / tell anyone that I applied for a new job.

6. And then he said / told to me, "Don't panic! Everything will be fine."

6 Changing adverbs and pronouns. Welche Angaben ändern sich in der indirekten Rede?

Alain: "I'm meeting the vice president this afternoon in Torquay."

– Alain said **1.** .... was meeting the vice president **2.** .... afternoon in Torquay.

Sara: "I thought you were going to meet him in Plymouth."

– Sara said **3.** .... thought **4.** .... were going to meet in Plymouth.

Alain: "We'll probably talk for an hour and then go out for dinner there."

– Alain replied **5.** .... would probably talk for an hour and then go out for dinner **6.** ....

> Je nachdem, wann, wo und von wem eine direkte Rede wiederholt wird, müssen sowohl die Personal- und Possessivpronomen als auch die Angaben von Ort und Zeit angepasst werden.

7 Expressions of time. Wie verändern sich gegebenenfalls die Zeitangaben?

1. today $\longrightarrow$ ....

2. tonight $\longrightarrow$ ....

3. yesterday $\longrightarrow$ ....

4. tomorrow $\longrightarrow$ ....

5. next week $\longrightarrow$ ....

6. last night $\longrightarrow$ ....

7. now $\longrightarrow$ ....

8. this $\longrightarrow$ ....

8 Indirect orders. Wie heißen die Verben richtig?

1. Paul **sadek** .... me to turn on the air-conditioning.

2. Karen **narwed** .... her sister not to take out another loan.

3. Greg **dotl** .... me to find a more inexpensive freight forwarder.

4. Samantha **gebged** .... her colleague not to leave the company.

5. The sergeant **redored** .... the privates to stop bickering.

> Indirekte Befehle erfolgen häufig mit folgenden Wendungen:
> *to ask sb. to do sth.*   jmdn. bitten, etw. zu tun
> *to tell sb. to do sth.*   jmdn. auffordern, etw. zu tun
> *to order sb. to do sth.*   jmdn. befehlen, etw. zu tun
> *to warn sb. not do do sth.*   jmdn. warnen, etw. (nicht) zu tun

9 Advise/advice. Setzen Sie die Satzteile zusammen.

1. ☐ We strongly advise you not to   **a)** changing money on the street.

2. ☐ They advised us against   **b)** that all employees take out a disability insurance.

3. ☐ I'd advise buying   **c)** go through the park alone at night.

4. ☐ It is strongly advised   **d)** us how to proceed from here.

5. ☐ They advise the company   **e)** government bonds instead of stocks.

6. ☐ He'll contact us later to advise   **f)** their lawyer's advice.

7. ☐ I think the agency should follow   **g)** to take the consultancy's advice.

8. ☐ He recommended the firm   **h)** on foreign investments.

> Das Verb *to advise* bedeutet *raten, beraten, empfehlen* sowie
> *abraten* mit der Negation *not* und der Präposition *against*.
> Das Substantiv schreibt man im *Br* mit -c: *advice*.

10 Indirect questions. Setzen Sie die Wörter an der richtigen Stelle ein.

how   where   if (2x)   who   how many   whether (2x)

1. The PA wasn't sure .... the board had decided in favour of the project.

2. The caller wanted to know .... the meeting is supposed to take place.

3. The secretary didn't want to tell me .... the Chinese delegation had decided to stay for another night or leave later this afternoon.

4. They asked me .... I would prevent the prices from falling.

5. Do you know .... the director has already left for the airport?

6. I was still wondering .... on earth would be so stupid as to leave the safe open after putting in confidential files.

7. Jack called because he wasn't sure .... people the catering should be for.

8. It's still unclear .... the wallet was lost or stolen.

> Indirekte Fragen werden mit *if* oder *whether* gebildet, die beide mit *ob* übersetzt werden, wobei *whether* eher dann verwendet wird, wenn von einer Wahl zwischen zwei oder mehreren Optionen die Rede ist. Indirekte Fragen können auch mit einem Fragepronomen eingeleitet werden, jedoch nicht mit einer Form von *to do*.

11 Mistakes. Finden Sie einen Fehler pro Satz.

1. She said she would wrote the minutes tomorrow.

2. They replied that production will start at the beginning of next year.

3. The reporter asked me if do I could tell him more about the scandal.

4. The department head told me set up a crisis committee as soon as possible.

5. The minister said me that house prices in Britain were rising again.

6. The line manager asked the trainee to buying some sandwiches.

7. He still didn't know whether the company is going to relocate or not.

1 Active or passive? Steht der Satz im Aktiv oder Passiv?

	Aktiv	Passiv
1. The company has been taken over by a Japanese corporation.	☐	☐
2. The two CEOs met in Tokyo yesterday morning.	☐	☐
3. The contract will probably be signed next week.	☐	☐
4. The company's shares are expected to rise.	☐	☐
5. It is feared that up to 1000 employees will be made redundant.	☐	☐
6. Union leaders already announced tough negotiations.	☐	☐

Passivsätze drücken aus, was mit einer Person oder Sache geschieht, wobei der Verursacher oftmals nicht erwähnt wird. Das im Deutschen verwendete Verb *werden* entspricht im Englischen einer Form von *to be*. Die nur in *Present* und *Past tense* mögliche *ing-Form* (*is/are being – was/were being*) teilt mit, dass etwas momentan – in der Gegenwart oder Vergangenheit – getan wird.

2 To be-Forms. Übersetzen Sie die Verbform ins Englische.

1. The firm wurde .... established in 1898 by my grandfather.

2. The shop wird ... werden .... closed at the end of the month.

3. More than 10 000 cars werden .... sold every month.

4. 100 employees sind ... worden .... laid off this year so far.

5. All entrances wurden .... locked by the facility manager last night.

6. The old factory wird gerade .... refurbished at the moment.

3 Activity or no activity? Welche Verbform ist richtig?

1. The Japanese acquired / were acquired the firm two months ago.

2. I had just promoted / had just been promoted to head of department.

3. After the takeover, the CEO would retired / was retired with a golden handshake.

4. The company had to / had been to recall a million items because of faulty parts.

5. The caretaker didn't leave / hadn't been left the door open when he left the office.

6. The road works will finish / will be finished by January next year at the latest.

4 Two objects. Sind beide Passivsätze korrekt? Kreuzen Sie die richtigen Sätze an.

1. The company awarded him £1000 for best sales representative.

    a) ☐ He was awarded £1000 for best sales representative.

    b) ☐ Him was awarded £1000 for best sales representative.

2. I mailed them the information pack yesterday morning.

    a) ☐ The information pack was mailed to them yesterday morning.

    b) ☐ They were mailed the information pack yesterday morning.

3. My colleagues bought me a nice bouquet of flowers for my 40th birthday.

    a) ☐ Me was bought a nice bouquet of flowers by my colleagues.

    b) ☐ I was bought a nice bouquet of flowers by my colleagues.

4. The line manager gave us some confidential information.

    a) ☐ We were given some confidential information by the line manager.

    b) ☐ Some confidential information was given to us by the line manager.

Im englischen Passivsatz wird das deutsche Dativpronomen (*mir/ihm/uns* usw.) zum Nominativ (*I/he/we* etc.):
Mir wurde gesagt, dass ...   *I* was told that ...
Uns wurde geraten (nicht) zu ...   *We* were advised (not) to...

5 Passive with preposition. Setzen Sie eine Präposition ein.

1. The merger contract will be looked .... by three attorneys.

2. It was announced on the radio that the concert is sold ....

3. The new offer has also been turned .... by the Russians.

4. The office complex was broken .... last night.

5. The new trainee was prevented .... showing her real potential.

6. All industries should be banned .... dumping plastic waste into the ocean.

6 Match-up. Verbinden Sie die Satzteile.

1. ☐ Hundreds of new breweries   **a)** inform you about our new products.

2. ☐ The briefing is supposed to   **b)** by the board of directors last week.

3. ☐ The decision was made   **c)** donated to a charity organization.

4. ☐ The money will be   **d)** were launched in the UK last year.

7 **Active or passive?** Übersetzen Sie die Sätze ins Englische.

1. Das neue Werk wird nächstes Jahr gebaut werden.

....

2. Die Methode wurde 2002 von dem damaligen Generaldirektor eingeführt.

....

3. Der Vizepräsident des belgischen Unternehmens ist gefeuert worden.

....

4. Der Manager soll £ 200 000 unterschlagen haben. (to embezzle)

....

8 **Active-passive mix-up.** Setzen Sie das Verb in der richtigen Form ein.

Do you know that we **1.** to be .... at our Tokyo subsidiary last week?

We **2.** to show around .... the premises for some time,

3. to listen .... to some talks

and **4.** to invite .... for dinner.

We **5.** to start .... the evening

at a *tachinomi* – one of Japan's famous

standing bars – and later **6.** to go ....

to a sushi restaurant. Have you ever

7. to eat .... authentic sushi? The food we **8.** to serve ....

was absolutely fantastic.

9 Indirect passive. Entscheiden Sie, welche Form richtig ist.

1. It expects / is expected that the company is going to move to Glasgow soon.

2. She rumoured / was rumoured to have taken the £ 50 from the kitty (Kaffeekasse).

3. The assistant believed / was believed that all items had been sold.

4. The company said / is said to have sold its production plants to the Chinese.

Indirekte Wendungen können mit *man* ins Deutsche übersetzt werden.

10 Passive with get. Setzen Sie eine Form von *to get* ein.

1. My mobile phone wurde gestohlen .... yesterday.

2. I never müde werden .... of listening to the old boss's stories.

3. The burglar wurde gefasst .... when he tried to use the stolen credit card.

4. They swore they betranken sich nicht .... at the staff party.

5. The new PA wird heiraten .... on an ocean liner next week.

6. Luckily nobody wurde gebissen .... by the dogs on the premises.

Das englische Passiv macht keinen Unterschied zwischen einem Vorgangspassiv und einem Zustandspassiv. Ein Satz wie *She was married* lässt sich auf zweifache Art übersetzen:
  Vorgangspassiv: *Sie wurde verheiratet (von jemandem) = Sie heiratete ...*
  Zustandspassiv: *Sie war verheiratet.*
Um Missverständnisse zu vermeiden, wird vor allem in der gesprochenen Sprache die *to be-*Form des Vorgangspassivs mit einer Form von *to get* ersetzt.

11 Other translations of „werden". Setzen Sie das passende Verb in der richtigen Zeitform ein.

to turn (2x)   to become   to get   to go   to grow

1. She was so embarrassed that she .... red.

2. Berry wants .... a manager when he's grown up.

3. They thought he .... completely mad.

4. "Sorry, I'm ill. I can't make it today." – "Okay, ... well soon!"

5. I don't feel like going out all night anymore – I think I .... old.

6. When he heard the news about the fire he .... pale.

12 Passive with modals. Welche Form ist richtig?

1. The components cannot be / have been delivered until 15 June.

2. The new line manager must be / have been under 30 – he looks so young.

3. The new road should be / have been finished last month.

4. The secretary won't be / have been in her office when you called.

Lernkrimi

MANHATTAN MURDER

Autor: **Timothy Woods Palma**

Manhattan, New York: Eine Joggerin wird tot unter
der Williamsburg Bridge aufgefunden. Doch was hat
die unscheinbare junge Frau mit dem Geschäftsmann
Mekko Harjo zu tun? Detective Ted Quinlan ist neu
beim NYPD und ermittelt mit seiner Partnerin
Detective Emily Peters in dem Fall, der sie tief in den
Financial District von New York führt ...

Auszug aus Lernkrimi Kurzkrimi *Murderous Network,* ISBN 978-3-8174-1956-2.
Den vollständigen Lernkrimi können Sie kostenlos als PDF downloaden. Folgen Sie einfach dem Link im Vorwort.

Chapter 1: Wall Street

It is Thursday morning, and Detective Ted Quinlan walks quickly through the crowd. He is **approaching** his first destination of the day. In all directions are people of every shape, size and color. They are all scurrying to get where they need to go. Most of them wear **suits**. They **appear** out of taxi cabs and subway entrances. There are men selling things out of carts on the sidewalk: coffee, bagels, pretzels. It is rush hour, and this is Manhattan's financial district.

1 Unscramble the words. Bringen Sie die Buchstaben in die richtige Reihenfolge!

1. inasdetonti ....

3. merootp ....

2. aarpep ....

4. ulhseedc ....

"I'm not in Brooklyn anymore," Ted thinks to himself, looking up at the giant black tower of One Chase Manhattan Plaza. Today is only his fourth day on the job as an NYPD Detective. Before being **promoted**, he'd been on the force for nearly twenty years as a patrol officer in Flatbush, South Brooklyn. His wife, Dorona, and his two daughters are all very happy because the new position has a regular schedule and is safer and better paid. They might even be able to soon afford the summer house they've always dreamed of. However, this morning, here on Wall Street, Ted couldn't be further from a **cozy** mountain getaway.

On the thirty-second floor of One Chase Manhattan Plaza is the **headquarters** of a large multi-national corporation called Praxis Incorporated International, or PII for short. Detective Quinlan is downtown to see a man named Mekko Harjo, who works as an **executive** at PII. Harjo has recently become a suspect through material **evidence** in a homicide. Ted pushes through the **revolving doors** and enters the lobby. Inside, it is far less crowded than on the street and smells less like garbage. In fact, it smells like mint. Everything is clean. All the surfaces are shining. Yet, despite the relative calm, Ted feels uncomfortable. Wall Street, he has

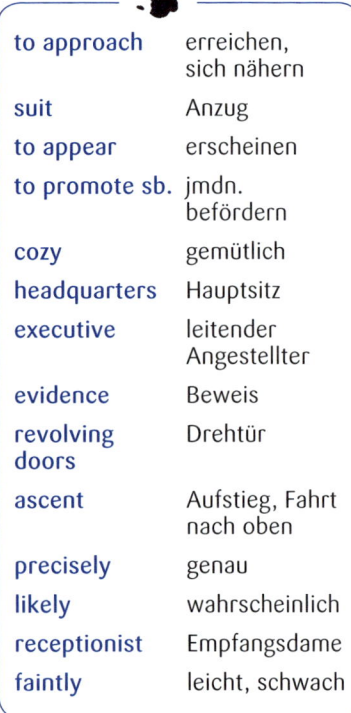

to approach	erreichen, sich nähern
suit	Anzug
to appear	erscheinen
to promote sb.	jmdn. befördern
cozy	gemütlich
headquarters	Hauptsitz
executive	leitender Angestellter
evidence	Beweis
revolving doors	Drehtür
ascent	Aufstieg, Fahrt nach oben
precisely	genau
likely	wahrscheinlich
receptionist	Empfangsdame
faintly	leicht, schwach

already realized, is a far more aggressive environment than any of the poor Brooklyn neighborhoods in which he has worked. He presses the button on the elevator, and there is a pleasant 'ding'. The doors open, and Detective Quinlan enters with a few others. He presses '32' and stands, a bit embarrassed. His suit is clearly of a lesser quality than those of the businessmen around him. The doors close, and they begin their ascent. As he has been doing incessantly for the past two days, Ted goes through the crime in his head:

Early Tuesday morning, a woman's body was discovered by a boat passing under the Williamsburg Bridge. She hadn't landed in the water, but instead on a concrete island at the bridge's base. Dressed in a pink track suit, the body remained, at first, unidentified.

This is precisely what happened. An hour later, a man in Brooklyn named Zeke Virant reported his girlfriend missing. He had woken up alone in bed and found a note on the kitchen counter from the night before: "Gone for a run!" She was likely wearing a pink track suit, he explained. Her name was Marjorie Schillo.

When the elevator arrives at the thirty-second floor, Ted steps out. He is surprised by what he sees. There is no one. It is just a large white and gray space, empty except for a fountain, a potted plant and three giant blue letters: PII. There is a set of frosted-glass doors, through which he can see the movement of silhouettes. They, too, are likely better dressed than he is. Ted pushes the doors open to find a receptionist behind a desk. She is young, with small features, glasses, and wears her brown hair pulled tightly back.

"Good morning, sir," she greets him. "How can I help you?"

Ted smiles back faintly and approaches the desk.

"I'm here to see Mr. Mekko Harjo," he tells her.

"Okay, sir, could I have your name?" she asks, still smiling. "Do you have an appointment with Mr. Harjo?"

2 Prepositions. Lesen Sie weiter und ergänzen Sie die fehlenden Präpositionen!

"This is often the case 1. .... runners," Ted had been told 2. ....

his new partner, Detective Emily Peters. She's a veteran NYPD Detective,

full 3. .... information, and happy 4. .... teach Ted her tricks 5. ....

the trade. "They usually go running without their wallets or cell phones,

so there is no form of I. D. We normally just need to wait 6. .... a missing person

report comes in."

"I'm Detective Ted Quinlan with the NYPD [i], and no, I don't have an appointment."

"Is Mr. Harjo expecting you?"

The detective shakes his head. "No."

Her eyes have grown wide and suspicious, and she begins to shift uncomfortably in her chair.

"Well, I'll let Mr. Harjo know that you're here. One moment, please."

Part of Ted is amused, but part of him feels guilty. The poor girl looks terrified. Perhaps she is new here. Or perhaps this is simply

> Das **New York City Police Department** (NYPD) ist der Polizeidienst von New York. Es besteht aus zehn Abteilungen. Die Polizisten des NYPD (zwischen 35.000 und 40.000 Vollzugsbeamte) werden übrigens auch als **New York's Finest** bezeichnet.

the first time a detective has ever come into the office of Praxis Incorporated International. Could it be? Ted hopes so. He would proudly be the first.

"Follow me," the receptionist tells Ted and leads him down a hallway to a door. She knocks and then opens it. Ted is taken aback by what he sees. The office is very bright, with floor-to-ceiling windows and a beautiful view of the harbor. Mekko Harjo rises from his desk to greet Detective Quinlan and shakes his hand.

"Good Morning, I'm Mekko Harjo."

"Detective Ted Quinlan. Pleasure."

"Please have a seat, Detective Quinlan," and Mekko gestures to the chair opposite his desk. But the movement causes him to wince, and he grabs his shoulder in pain. The receptionist closes the door behind her.

appointment	Termin
suspicious	misstrauisch
taken aback	verblüfft
wince	zusammen-zucken
attempt	versuchen
agitation	Aufregung
⚡ to play hardball	mit harten Bandagen kämpfen
to vanish	verschwinden
to recompose oneself	sich wieder fangen
lost for words	sprachlos
verify	überprüfen

"What can I do for you today, Detective?"

"I'm here to ask you about your relationship with Marjorie Schillo."

"Marjorie Schillo?"

"Yes, Marjorie Schillo."

Mekko pauses, as if uncomfortable to go on, but continues.

"Marjorie Schillo, the physicist?"

Ted attempts to hide his excitement. Would it be this easy?

"That's right, the physicist. So you do know her?"

"Yes. We went to university together."

Ted looks over Mekko's shoulder. On the wall, a diploma hangs: Columbia School of Business.

"And have you seen one another often since then?"

"Not often. We've kept in touch, here and there. We were friends."

"When was the last time you saw Ms. Schillo?"

Mekko's face begins to show a sort of agitation.

"I'm not entirely sure, detective. But may I ask you why you're in my office right now asking me about a relationship with an old classmate?"

"So he wants to play hardball," Ted thinks to himself.

"Where were you Monday evening, Mr. Harjo?"

"I was in Boston, on business."

"You spent the night there?"

"Yes. At the Intercontinental Hotel. Why?"

"Well, Mr. Harjo, Marjorie Schillo was found dead two days ago, and it's looking increasingly like homicide."

Harjo's face drops, and for the moment his building aggression vanishes. It takes a moment for him to recompose himself and continue.

"That's very sad," he says, seeming genuine. "But, detective, what do I have to do with it?"

"Because, Mr. Harjo, we found a note in her pocket signed 'Mekko', telling her to meet him on Monday night, only hours before she was found dead."

Mekko swallows. For a moment, he is lost for words.

"I don't know what to tell you. I know nothing about it."

Ted stands up. "Well, if you can think of anything to tell me, here's my card. And if you wouldn't mind, I'd like to call the Intercontinental in Boston, in order to verify your stay there."

Mekko rises as well, and they shake hands like they had when Ted entered. Only this time, Mekko isn't smiling.

3 Unscramble the sentences. Bringen Sie die Wörter in die richtige Reihenfolge!

1. building   for   aggression   moment   the   vanishes   his

....

2. what   not   to   you   do   tell   I   know

....

3. found   pocket   her   in   we   note   a

....

4. across   by   quickest   the   river   ferry   is   the   way

....

"Y-Yes," he half stutters, "feel free to contact them."
Ted nods, eyes fixed on the suspect. "Can I ask you one more question, Mr. Harjo? It seems as if you've hurt your shoulder. How did that happen?"
Mekko puts his hand to his injured shoulder and nods **affirmatively**.
"It's from a sailing accident last weekend in Montauk."
Quinlan nods. "Have a good day, Mr. Harjo."
"You too," Harjo responds and sits back down. He stares **blankly** out the window. As he closes the door behind him, Ted can see shimmers of the late morning sun on the river.
Walking away from One Manhattan Plaza, he is excited to be returning to his **precinct** in Williamsburg. He has a meeting over lunch with his partner Emily, who has just spoken to the victim's boyfriend Zeke Virant, and the quickest way across the river is by ferry.

affirmatively	zustimmend, bejahend
blankly	ausdruckslos
precinct	**hier:** Polizeirevier
spot	Ort, Stelle
gut instinct	Bauchgefühl
to come forward	**hier:** sich stellen
to capitulate	aufgeben, sich ergeben

Chapter 2: The Bridge

The ferry pulls away from the dock at Wall Street and passes through the same sparkling harbor waters that Mekko Harjo can see from his office window. Perhaps Mekko's still looking down, Ted thinks to himself. He uses the free moment to call his secretary. He tells her about the Boston flight and hotel information and asks her to request verification.
Before long, the ferry is passing under the Williamsburg Bridge, right near the **spot** where the body of Marjorie Schillo had landed. Police tape still hangs on the concrete island. Ted looks up at the spot from where she must have jumped, or was thrown. But, if thrown, by who **i**?
He thinks back to only two days ago, Tuesday morning, when he stood there with his new partner investigating his very first crime scene as a NYPD Detective. He remembers their conversation:
"Do you think it's a suicide?" Ted had asked Emily, as they walked away from the crime scene and down the bridge towards their car. She shook her head.
"My **gut instinct** tells me no, but there's no evidence in either direction yet. Forensics will

Im amerikanischen Englisch wird oft **who** statt anstelle des Objektpronomens whom verwendet. Nach **by, for, with** steht normalerweise **whom**, aber **who** ist nicht immer unkorrekt.

collect DNA samples from her clothes and from beneath her fingernails. But we also don't have any witnesses."
"You don't think that anyone will **come forward**?"
"Three-fourths of all witnesses step forth within the first few hours following a crime. So if no one has yet, there's only a small chance anyone will."

Ted was curious. "What about the other one-fourth?"

"They don't come forward at all, usually out of fear. They don't want to be the next victim, or they just don't want to get involved." Ted nodded.

"Especially in a city like New York," Emily continued. "People just want to be left alone."

They were interrupted by a voice coming out from beside a garbage can, where a homeless man sat holding a hamburger.

"Did you find him?" the man asked.

Ted responded. "Find who?"

"The guy in the purple trench coat," the man replied with a grin. "The one that was screaming at the woman last night."

Emily glanced quickly at Ted and then back to the man.

"What time last night?" she asked. "What did you see?"

His smile went away and he suddenly seemed angry. "Well if I tell you, what do I get out of it? Cops have never been nothing but trouble for me."

"We're not cops," Ted interjected. "We're detectives, and if you don't cooperate, we'll have to take you into the precinct. You're a witness to a possible homicide." He kneeled down towards the man. "So we hope you'll tell us what you saw."

The man capitulated. He didn't want any trouble.

"Well, it was pretty late, and I was sitting here, and I heard a woman's scream first, then a man's."

"What time was it?" Emily asked.

"Oh, I don't know," he said, motioning to his empty wrist. "I don't exactly got a watch."

4 Past Tense. Lesen Sie weiter und setzen Sie die Verben ins Simple Past.

"**1.** Do .... you see the woman?" asked Emily.

The man **2.** shake .... his head. "No, by the time I **3.** get .... up to look,

she was gone. I don't know where she **4.** go ....; she sort of disappeared."

"But you **5.** see .... the man?" Ted asked.

"Only from behind. He **6.** wear .... a big purple trench coat and a big black hat

and was walking down that way, pretty quickly."

"Towards Manhattan," Ted confirmed. The man **7.** nod ....

"Thank you very much for your help," **8.** say .... Ted with a smile.

"Approximately what time," Ted amended sternly.

The man looked up to the sky, thinking. "Oh, I'd say, midnight."

They began to walk away, but Ted turned around.

"What's your name, sir?" he asked. The identity of a witness can make or break a case.

He smiled crazily. "The name's Richard Gluski." He took a big bite out of his hamburger. "But you can call me Ricky!"

"Richard Gluski," Ted repeated to himself, and they walked away, heading back to the precinct.

A few hours later, the coroner called. He informed them that he had found signs of a struggle: namely bruising on the victim's neck.

"They seem to be from strangling," he explained.

"Were they masculine hands?" Ted asked, hoping for a push in the right direction.

"I'd say so," the coroner responded. "They aren't small."

At midnight, a strangling. A man, in a purple trench coat.

The bridge had no video surveillance, and the only witness was Ricky, the homeless man. Ted feared the

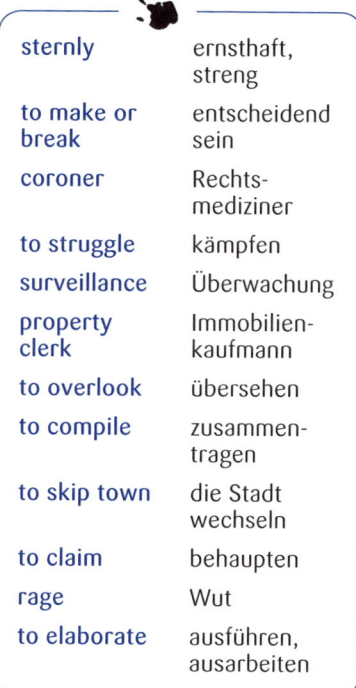

sternly	ernsthaft, streng
to make or break	entscheidend sein
coroner	Rechts-mediziner
to struggle	kämpfen
surveillance	Überwachung
property clerk	Immobilien-kaufmann
to overlook	übersehen
to compile	zusammen-tragen
to skip town	die Stadt wechseln
to claim	behaupten
rage	Wut
to elaborate	ausführen, ausarbeiten

case would go nowhere. But the next day, Wednesday afternoon, Ted received a call from the property clerk that set the case in motion:

"Detective Quinlan, this is Richie Halter, from Properties."

"How can I help you, Richie?"

"I've got some good news for you, detective. It seems as if you overlooked a hidden pocket in the pink track suit of Marjorie Schillo. We were packaging it up for evidence when we found a note. I think it will help you out, big time."

Ted became excited. "What did it say, Richie?"

"It said, 'My very dear Marjorie, meet me Monday night, same spot. Love, Mekko.'"

Bingo!

The detectives couldn't have asked for a more helpful name. There were only three Mekkos registered in New York City, and two of them were children.

So they had a suspect: Mekko Harjo.

Over lunch, Ted is feeling refreshed from the ferry ride across the river. He and Emily discuss all the information they've compiled thus far. Emily eats kale and miso soup as usual and tells Ted about the phone conversation she's just had with Zeke Virant, the boyfriend. He's not in New York, but in Pittsburgh.

"So he has already skipped town," remarks Ted. "Strange, isn't it?"

"He said he was with the Schillo family, preparing the funeral services. He told me he's practically part of the family. They'd been together nearly twenty years." Ted nods.

"But here's the thing," Emily continues. "When I mentioned the name Mekko, he acted very bizarrely."

"Bizarre, how?"

"Well, he began to stutter and seemed angry. And then he refused to speak any further, told me he was too busy and hung up."

"So you think he knows something?"

"Well his tone was undoubtedly defensive."

Ted pauses. "He didn't say anything about knowing Harjo?"

"Knowing Harjo?" Emily is surprised by the question. "No, he didn't. You think Virant and Harjo know one another?"

"Well, Harjo told me that he went to Columbia with Marjorie, and that they were old friends."

"Really? But he didn't write the note?"

Ted shakes his head. "No, or at least he claims he didn't. But, if Mekko and Marjorie were having an affair, that would explain why the name Mekko got Virant all upset."

"True," Emily acknowledges.

"Do you think maybe he found out? Maybe he is the guy in the trench coat. A homicide of jealous rage?"

"We don't know enough yet," Emily says, "but we should keep our eyes open. Zeke is the last one to see Marjorie alive, and he's also the only one who seems to be withholding information. Unless you got something else out of Harjo?"

Ted puts down the ham and cheese sandwich Dorona made him and elaborates for Emily about his meeting with Mekko at the PII office. He mentions Mekko's injured arm.

"An injured arm," Emily repeats. "That's very interesting. It would make sense that, if there was a struggle like the coroner said, the man might have been injured too."

"Did Zeke have any apparent injuries?"

Emily shakes her head. "Not that I noticed, no."

5 **Definitions.** Verbinden Sie die Wörter mit ihren Definitionen!

1. ☐ come forward   a) engage in conflict

2. ☐ give in   b) make oneself known

3. ☐ struggle   c) refuse to give

4. ☐ withhold   d) surrender

6 **True or false?** Sind die folgenden Aussagen korrekt?
Markieren Sie mit richtig ✔ oder falsch ✘!

1. Ted is a veteran detective.

2. Detectives Quinlan and Peters do not get along.

3. The witness on the bridge was not immediately helpful.

4. Zeke went home to Pittsburgh to see his family.

5. Mekko lives uptown.

Ted's phone rings, and he picks it up. It is his secretary, and the news is disappointing. Emily can read it on his face.
"What's wrong?" she asks him.
"The hotel in Boston supports Harjo's alibi," he tells her. "He checked in at 7pm Monday evening and checked out Tuesday morning. United Airlines, too, verifies his presence on both flights."
"So he couldn't have been in New York at the time of the murder."
"Anything is possible," Ted says, shrugging, "But as far as evidence is concerned, Harjo was out of town. We would need to find further evidence, somewhere else."

trapped	gefangen
rarely	selten

The two sit there in silence, digesting their meals and considering their options.
"Next step?" Emily asks, a bit **trapped** in all the information.
"I suppose the only place to go is uptown."
Emily nods in agreement. "To Harjo's house."
So, Detectives Peters and Quinlan leave the precinct for their car. They're headed over the bridge and past the crime scene, then northbound up the FDR Drive, towards a place the two **rarely** go: the Upper East Side.

Mit **FDR-Drive** (oder auch **The Drive**) ist der ca. 15 km lange **Franklin D. Roosevelt East River Drive** gemeint, der an der East Side von Manhattan entlang des East River verläuft.

PHRASEN UND WORTSCHATZ

Sich und andere vorstellen

1 1. are 2. about 3. meet 4. Nice 5. call 6. speak
2 1. Woher kommen Sie? 2. Was tun Sie (beruflich)? 3. In welcher Branche sind Sie tätig?
   4. Was für ein Unternehmen ist das? 5. Wann sind Sie angekommen?
3 1. meet 2. introduce 3. introduce 4. introduced 5. this is 6. introduce 7. name is 8. met
4 1. management 2. electronics 3. business relations 4. hospitality 5. experience
5 1. c 2. a 3. d 4. e 5. b
6 body language, politeness, gestures, personal space, clothes
7 1. work 2. in charge 3. report 4. manage/supervise 5. involves 6. responsible 7. do
8 1. I'm staying at a very nice hotel not far from the city centre. 2. The flight was okay, but the food
   could have been better. 3. Thanks for sending someone to pick me up at the airport. 4. I'm suffering
   a bit from jet lag, but I'll feel better tomorrow morning. 5. Thanks for your offer, but I think I'll take
   a taxi.
9 1. rudeness 2. fresh 3. roommate 4. holidays 5. campsite
10 1. To my right 2. welcome 3. has arrived 4. will be helping out 5. by the way 6. say hello to
   7. until the end of the month
11 1. firm handshake 2. exchanged handshakes 3. warm and hearty 4. limp handshake
   5. on a handshake
12 1. excellent 2. beautiful 3. excited 4. positive 5. meeting 6. interested
13 1. I've never been to Manchester. 2. I'll be/I'm staying in London for three days. 3. I've just arrived
   from the airport. 4. The hotel is very nice and comfortable.

Firmen und Firmenhierarchie

1 1. corporation (Corp.) 2. subsidiary 3. firm 4. combine 5. company (Co.)
2 1. e 2. d 3. f 4. c 5. a 6. b   Lösung: public
3 1. joint 2. cooperatives 3. merger 4. takeover 5. association 6. enterprise
4 1. c 2. b 3. b 4. a
5 1. specialize in 2. provides 3. was founded in 4. has been selling/sold 5. has always operated/
   always operates 6. employs 7. is/was based in
6 1. managing director 2. financial director 3. head of human resources 4. production manager
   5. sales manager 6. head of accounting
7 Waagerecht: workmate, staff member, intern, employee;
   Senkrecht: trainee, worker
8 1. accounts 2. public relations 3. human resources 4. manufacturing 5. research and development
   6. sales 7. board of directors
9 1. customer service department 2. import-export company/firm 3. marketing department
   4. car company 5. stress 6. income

Telefonieren

1 Reihenfolge: 7-6-8-5-4-2-1-3
2 1. d 2. c 3. a 4. b 5. g 6. f 7. e
3 1. to speak 2. calling 3. this is 4. to leave 5. to call ... back 6. pass ... on

4 **1.** false, The caller wants to speak to Mr Jackson. **2.** false, The receptionist's name is Randolph Brown. **3.** false, She is calling from R&F. **4.** true **5.** false, The caller asks for Mr Jackson's call. **6.** false, The receptionist will pass on the message after the meeting.

5 **1.** cordless phone **2.** mobile/cell phone **3.** public phone **4.** hands-free phone **5.** answering machine **6.** vintage telephone

6 **1.** c **2.** d **3.** a **4.** f **5.** b **6.** g **7.** e

7 **1.** in **2.** at **3.** on **4.** out **5.** at **6.** on **7.** from **8.** on

8 **1.** Entschuldigung, wer ist am Apparat? **2.** Darf ich fragen, um was es geht? **3.** Könnten Sie Ihren Namen bitte buchstabieren? **4.** Möchten Sie dranbleiben? **5.** Einen Moment, bitte, ich verbinde.

9 **1.** department **2.** from **3.** ask **4.** message **5.** have **6.** write

10 **1.** f **2.** d **3.** e **4.** b **5.** c **6.** a

11 **1.** rings **2.** answer **3.** finish **4.** put **5.** hang up on **6.** saying

12 **1.** This is a message for Mr Thorvaldson. **2.** I have called you at least five times. **3.** I'm sorry I have to cancel our meeting on Friday morning. **4.** Please pass that message on to him. **5.** I'm out of town until tomorrow afternoon. **6.** You should see my number on your display. **7.** Please get in touch with me as soon as possible.

13 **1.** b **2.** d **3.** e **4.** c **5.** a

14 **1.** return this call **2.** This is/It's Mark from **3.** postpone … until **4.** extension **5.** 4 p.m. **6.** if you're still there

15 **1.** connection **2.** phone number **3.** battery **4.** area code **5.** emergency call **6.** extension **7.** no reception   **Lösung:** charger

16 **1.** speaking **2.** repeat **3.** spell **4.** I'm afraid **5.** hold **6.** calling

17 **1.** o o one seven eight one **2.** o o four four one four three

E-Mailen

1 **1.** b **2.** c **3.** c **4.** b **5.** c **6.** c **7.** a **8.** b

2 **1.** to enquire **2.** if **3.** hoping **4.** grateful **5.** interested in **6.** let me know **7.** contacting

3 **1.** opening salutation **2.** introduction **3.** reason for writing **4.** closing sentence **5.** closing salutation **6.** sender's name

4 **1.** f **2.** d **3.** e **4.** a **5.** c **6.** b

5 **1.** for **2.** to **3.** from **4.** in

6 **1.** Yours faithfully **2.** Yours sincerely **3.** Regards **4.** Best wishes **5.** All the best **6.** Love

7 1, 4, 5, 6

8 **1.** offer **2.** order **3.** company **4.** discount **5.** goods **6.** receipt **7.** Payment **8.** confirmation

9 **1.** trial **2.** repeat **3.** on call **4.** advance **5.** rush **6.** standing

10

	Englisch	Deutsch
1. re.	referring	bezüglich, bzgl.
2. FYI	For Your Information	zu Ihrer Information
3. P.A.	Personal Assistant	persönliche(r) Assistent(in)
4. e.g.	for example	zum Beispiel, z.B.
5. FAO	For the Attention Of	zu Händen von, z.H(d).
6. i.e.	that is	das heißt, d.h.
7. no.	number	Nummer, Nr.
8. approx.	approximately	ungefähr
9. c/o	care of	wohnhaft bei

11 **Reihenfolge:** 5-4-6-2-1-3

12 **1.** received **2.** inform **3.** charge **4.** absent **5.** apologies **6.** understanding

13 **1.** (communication) cable **2.** external hard drive **3.** headset **4.** USB (memory) stick
 5. keyboard **6.** CD drive **7.** mouse **8.** SD card

14 **1.** a **2.** b **3.** c **4.** b **5.** c **6.** a **7.** b

15 **1.** speichern **2.** herunterladen **3.** kopieren **4.** öffnen **5.** löschen **6.** anhängen **7.** erstellen
 8. hochladen **9.** schließen

16 **1.** from **2.** in **3.** over **4.** on **5.** on **6.** to

Termine

1 **1.** behalf **2.** appointment **3.** diary **4.** meeting **5.** office **6.** calling

2 **1.** make **2.** keep **3.** postpone **4.** cancel **5.** get **6.** confirm **7.** have **8.** miss

3 **1.** c **2.** a **3.** e **4.** b **5.** d **6.** g **7.** f

4 **1.** available/free **2.** suit **3.** make **4.** possible **5.** see **6.** convenient/possible **7.** free/available

5 **1.** I'm afraid/sorry **2.** postpone **3.** can't make **4.** can't manage **5.** be free **6.** available
 7. understanding

6 **1.** e **2.** d **3.** f **4.** a **5.** b **6.** c

7 **Waagerecht: 1.** reschedule **2.** attend **3.** deadline **4.** call off **5.** arrange;
 Senkrecht: 6. diary **7.** keep **8.** finish

8 **1.** I have/need to cancel my appointment with you. **2.** I can't keep the appointment at 2 p.m.
 3. I'm awfully sorry that I missed our appointment. **4.** I had an urgent appointment with my lawyer.
 5. I would like to arrange/make/fix/set up a new appointment.

Bürokorrespondenz

1 **1.** letter head **2.** addressee **3.** date **4.** salutation **5.** reference **6.** body (of the letter)
 7. closing sentence(s) **8.** closing salutation **9.** signature block

2 **1.** d **2.** c **3.** a **4.** f **5.** b **6.** e

3 **1.** forward **2.** grateful **3.** obliged **4.** appreciate **5.** delighted

4 **1.** As **2.** on **3.** by **4.** for

5 **1.** d **2.** c **3.** a **4.** b **5.** f **6.** e

6 **1.** As stated **2.** As you will see from **3.** as per

7 **1.** thank you **2.** look forward **3.** trust **4.** pleased **5.** certain **6.** receive **7.** meet **8.** make ... effort

8 **1.** are pleased to **2.** is with pleasure **3.** Please let us know **4.** take pleasure in

9 **1.** for **2.** for **3.** that **4.** for **5.** have **6.** that

10 **1.** (cash) **2.** volume/bulk/quantity **3.** introductory **4.** wholesale **5.** loyalty **6.** import

11 **1.** Rechnungsnummer **2.** Kundennummer **3.** Steuernummer **4.** Datum **5.** Nettopreis
 6. Zwischensumme **7.** Value Added Tax = Umsatzsteuer (Mehrwertsteuer) **8.** Gesamtsumme

12 **1.** remitted **2.** make **3.** accepts **4.** settle **5.** overdraw

13 **1.** the nineteenth of April two thousand eighteen **2.** September 8(th) twenty-ten
 3. ten thousand and eight hundred yen **4.** three hundred million **5.** o point six six/two thirds
 6. five point five percent

14 **1.** in **2.** by **3.** on **4.** on **5.** in

15 **1.** Konto **2.** Kontoinhaber(in) **3.** Einzugsermächtigung/Lastschriftverfahren **4.** Dauerauftrag

16 **1.** samples **2.** agreed **3.** dozen **4.** enclosed **5.** fortnight **6.** return

17 **1.** matter **2.** mistake **3.** rectify **4.** dissatisfied **5.** reimburse **6.** charged

18 **1.** overdue **2.** oversights **3.** outstanding **4.** submitted **5.** disregard
19 **1.** information pack **2.** sales literature **3.** price list **4.** catalogue **5.** magazine **6.** brochure
7. leaflet **8.** flyer

Arbeitsroutine

1 **1.** folders **2.** pen **3.** notebook **4.** lamp **5.** smartphone/mobile/cell phone
6. chair **7.** clip board **8.** desk
2 **1.** e **2.** g **3.** a **4.** h **5.** b **6.** d **7.** c **8.** f
3 **1.** mug **2.** plant **3.** copier **4.** printer **5.** fax machine **6.** coffee maker **7.** filing cabinet
8. waste-paper basket
4 **1.** run out of **2.** to order **3.** printed out **4.** informed **5.** file **6.** turn on **7.** emptied **8.** to buy
5 **1.** cups of coffee **2.** milk and sugar **3.** spill **4.** coffee stains **5.** make **6.** pour **7.** strong
8. decaf(feinated coffee)
6 **1.** taken care of **2.** label **3.** type up **4.** Listen to **5.** proofread **6.** arrange
7 meeting, colleagues, agenda, minutes, whiteboard, conference room, canteen, swivel chair
8 **1.** a **2.** b **3.** a **4.** b **5.** a **6.** b
9 **1.** Have you (already) posted the letter to Mr Anthony? **2.** Has the post arrived yet?
3. I'll put the letter in the post tomorrow. **4.** It's better to have the letter registered.
5. The parcel arrived through the post.
10 **1.** e **2.** a **3.** f **4.** b **5.** d **6.** c
11 **1.** at/on **2.** of **3.** with **4.** in **5.** on
12 **1.** on the train **2.** commutes **3.** walking distance **4.** company car **5.** rush-hour traffic
13 **1.** b **2.** a **3.** c **4.** a **5.** c
14 **Mögliche Antworten: 1.** I do a lot of paperwork and I seem to be on the phone all day.
2. I like organizing things. I think I'm a very structured person. And I like talking to other people.
3. I usually work 38 hours a week, but sometimes I have to work overtime.
15 **1.** trained **2.** training **3.** training **4.** trainee **5.** training **6.** training **7.** trained **8.** trained
16 **1.** a three-year apprenticeship **2.** as an apprentice electrician **3.** was apprenticed to
4. for an apprenticeship **5.** to take on apprentices **6.** finding apprentices
17 **1.** in **2.** home **3.** happen **4.** reach **5.** office **6.** telling
18 Q: So, you've **started** working from home. What's the difference between working from home
and working in an **office**?
A: First of all, I'm a lot **more** relaxed. I don't have to dress up in the morning. I don't even have to
get up at all, if I don't **feel** like it ..., well as least not as early as during the rest of the week. I can
drink as much tea as I like while working and can even have a **snack** sitting next to my laptop.
Nobody is **complaining** when I decide to take half an hour **off** to read the newspaper or pop round
to the shop to get something to eat.
Q: What is the minimum requirement for working from home in **terms** of equipment?
A: It almost goes without saying that I need fast **internet**, a good broadband connection is a basic
requirement for my kind of **work**. But other than that ..., I have all the programs I need on my
laptop. So I feel pretty **independent**.

Konferenzen und Präsentationen

1   **1.** crisis meeting – Krisensitzung **2.** emergency meeting – Dringlichkeitssitzung
    3. board meeting – Vorstandssitzung **4.** special meeting – Sondersitzung **5.** staff meeting –
    Belegschaftssitzung, Mitarbeiterbesprechung **6.** committee meeting – Ausschusssitzung
2   **1.** to open **2.** to depart in **3.** to guest **4.** to detain **5.** to cancel
3   **1.** holding **2.** solve **3.** take **4.** raised **5.** made **6.** taking **7.** reach **8.** hold
4   **1.** brainstorming session **2.** briefing **3.** progress report **4.** budget
5   **1.** write **2.** take care of **3.** carried **4.** deal with **5.** take
6   **1.** debate **2.** argument **3.** discussion **4.** negotiations **5.** talks
7   **1.** with **2.** more **3.** to **4.** was **5.** what **6.** up
8   **1.** c **2.** e **3.** d **4.** b **5.** a
9   **1.** sich weigern **2.** uneins/nicht einig sein **3.** nicht übereinstimmen mit
    4. nicht zustimmen, anderer Meinung sein **5.** geteilter Meinung sein in **6.** etw. nicht einhalten
10 **1.** out **2.** to **3.** on **4.** on **5.** up with **6.** at
11 **1.** I might be wrong, but ... **2.** It seems to me that ... **3.** In my opinion ...
    4. As far as I'm concerned ... **5.** Well, if you ask me ...
12 **1.** pie chart **2.** bar chart **3.** line chart **4.** organization chart **5.** area chart **6.** table
13 **1.** b **2.** d **3.** a **4.** c
14 **1.** title **2.** x-axis **3.** y-axis **4.** bars **5.** graph **6.** (sales) figures **7.** years
15 **1.** have **2.** give **3.** received **4.** turn **5.** pay
16 **1.** by **2.** of **3.** about **4.** to **5.** in

Smalltalk

1   **1.** family **2.** work **3.** sport **4.** holidays   **Lösung:** food
2   **1.** Are you interested in modern art? **2.** Do you prefer coffee or tea? **3.** Did you have a good flight?
    4. Do you like watching sport(s)? **5.** What kind of food do you like? **6.** Have you been here before?
    7. How do you like our town/city?
3   **1.** sultry **2.** humid **3.** muggy **4.** fair **5.** mild **6.** hot **7.** bright
4   **1.** is **2.** seen **3.** more **4.** rain
5   **1.** d **2.** c **3.** a **4.** b
6   **1.** latest film **2.** scenery **3.** capturing **4.** love-hate relationship **5.** weather conditions **6.** affordable
    7. prices **8.** big screen
7   **1.** comedy, documentary, drama, thriller, adventure; **2.** love, can't stand, hate, enjoy, adore;
    3. interesting, bad, entertaining, awful, mainstream
8   **1.** for **2.** for **3.** as ... as **4.** round **5.** up **6.** from **7.** round
9   **1.** non-alcoholic beer **2.** draught beer **3.** shandy **4.** stout **5.** lager **6.** ale **7.** bitter   **Lösung:** cider
10 **1.** up **2.** loud **3.** somewhere **4.** watching **5.** hardly **6.** expect **7.** entertainment **8.** Let
11 **1.** Can you recommend something?/What do you recommend? **2.** The next round is on me.
    3. Do they serve food here?
12 **1.** socialize **2.** celebrate **3.** relationship
    Mögliche Antworten: 1. We meet once a month in a pub. **2.** Yes, we usually have a glass of
    champagne after work. **3.** No never. You shouldn't fall in love with a colleague.
13 **1.** c **2.** a **3.** b
14 **1.** Südafrika, 21. März **2.** Großbritannien, letzter Montag im Mai **3.** Irland und USA, 17. März
    4. Australien und Neuseeland, 25. April

Geschäftsreisen I: Im Hotel

1 **1.** reserve **2.** breakfast **3.** non-smoking **4.** balcony **5.** jet-lagged **6.** pick ... up **7.** shuttle service **8.** hearing

2 **1.** motel **2.** B&B **3.** 5-star hotel

3 **1.** breakfast buffet **2.** smoking lounge **3.** second floor **4.** tax **5.** flight information **6.** airport

4 **1.** reply **2.** change **3.** flight **4.** fully **5.** arriving **6.** scheduled

5 **1.** Ich muss die Reservierung stornieren **2.** Sie hatte einen Autounfall **3.** Lassen Sie mich im Computer nachschauen. **4.** so kurzfristig **5.** Sie ist völlig am Boden zerstört **6.** die Gebühr mit der Hotelrechnung verrechnen

6 **1.** ensuite bathroom **2.** lounge **3.** fitness room **4.** lobby/reception **5.** parking area **6.** sauna

7 **1.** wardrobe **2.** (Venetian) blind **3.** bedside table **4.** lampshade **5.** queen-size bed **6.** armchair **7.** walk-in closet

8 **1.** e **2.** a **3.** f **4.** g **5.** c **6.** d **7.** b

9 **1.** air-conditioning/TV **2.** toilet **3.** sheets/towels **4.** towels **5.** TV/air-conditioning

10 **1.** wi-fi **2.** password, pin, code **3.** access **4.** international calls

11 **1.** reservation **2.** identification **3.** passport **4.** keycard **5.** elevator **6.** bar **7.** aisle **8.** stay

12 **1.** check out **2.** luggage **3.** valuables **4.** debit card **5.** ironing service

Geschäftsreisen II: Unterwegs

1 **1.** first-class **2.** single ticket **3.** train **4.** platform **5.** underground fare **6.** tube ticket

2 **1.** b **2.** d **3.** a **4.** c

3 **1.** medium-sized **2.** driving licence **3.** sheet **4.** insurance **5.** tank

4 **1.** convertible **2.** hatchback **3.** estate car, (Am) station wagon **4.** sports car **5.** four-wheel drive/SUV **6.** saloon car, (Am sedan)

5 **1.** traffic lights **2.** lane **3.** roundabout **4.** ring road **5.** petrol station **6.** one-way street **7.** crossroads

6 **1.** Is there a hospital with a casualty department in the vicinity? **2.** Do you know a pub with local specialities around here? **3.** Where is the nearest garage? I've got a flat tyre.

7 **1.** tunnel **2.** overpass **3.** traffic jam

8 **1.** ready to order **2.** as a starter **3.** main course **4.** rare **5.** side order **6.** for dessert

9 **1.** menu **2.** wine list **3.** children's menu **4.** appealing **5.** meal **6.** complain **7.** side salad

10 **1.** fast-food **2.** fish **3.** romantic **4.** self-service **5.** four-star   **Lösung:** family diner

11 **Restaurant:** four-star, gourmet, high-end, posh;
Food: delicious, nutritious, organic, tasty;
Menu: cocktail, dessert, fixed-price, three-course

12 **1.** Can I have the bill, please? **2.** Can I pay by credit card? **3.** There seems to be a mistake on the bill. **4.** The restaurant bill came to £65 without tip. **5.** I asked the waiter to bring me the bill. **6.** We left a 15% (percent) tip on the table.

13 **1.** call **2.** nearest **3.** on **4.** off **5.** is **6.** over **7.** change

Bewerbungen und Vorstellungsgespräche

1 **1.** leading **2.** talented **3.** support **4.** represent **5.** include **6.** existing

2 **1.** profound **2.** large-scale **3.** hard-working **4.** ambitious **5.** foreign **6.** face-to-face

3 **1.** Objective **2.** Personal Information **3.** Education **4.** Professional Experience **5.** Skills **6.** Interests

4 **1.** advertised **2.** employed **3.** have gained **4.** working **5.** staging **6.** enclosed **7.** provide **8.** to discuss

5 **1.** advertised **2.** practical **3.** working **4.** trained **5.** placement **6.** knowledge **7.** notice **8.** opportunity

6 **1.** Ich habe Ihre Annonce für eine Anstellung als Versicherungskaufmann/-makler auf Ihrer Homepage gesehen. **2.** Nach dem Abitur habe ich eine Ausbildung zur/m Bürokauffrau/-kaufmann gemacht. **3.** Ich arbeite seit 2014 für eine führende Marketingfirma. **4.** Ich würde gern für ein(e) britische(s) Unternehmen/Firma arbeiten. **5.** Ich lege meinen Lebenslauf und ein Empfehlungs-schreiben bei.

7 **1.** b **2.** d **3.** e **4.** g **5.** h **6.** a **7.** c **8.** f

8 **1.** lack of confidence **2.** lack of preparation **3.** lack of career planning **4.** lack of enthusiasm **5.** poor grammar **6.** lack of interest **7.** limp handshake **8.** lack of courtesy   **Lösung:** focus on money

GRAMMATIK

Die Zeiten

1 **1.** starts **2.** working **3.** answer **4.** loves **5.** is writing **6.** is thinking **7.** wants

2 **1.** need **2.** is trying **3.** seems **4.** is doing **5.** are getting **6.** is expecting **7.** doesn't know **8.** think

3 **1.** am using **2.** cost **3.** is showing **4.** doesn't finish **5.** suppose

4 **1.** I hate having to write invoices all day. **2.** The insolvency of his main competitor/chief rival doesn't touch him at all. **3.** The whole matter/case/issue smells of corruption. **4.** I really dislike/don't like it when the CFO praises the company to the skies. **5.** I was hoping that my boss would retire at the end of the year.

5 **1.** c **2.** a **3.** b **4.** d

6 **1.** had **2.** was **3.** joined **4.** have never seen **5.** sat **6.** dared **7.** have talked **8.** haven't dealt

7 **1.** a **2.** a **3.** a **4.** b **5.** a **6.** b

8 **1.** for **2.** since **3.** since **4.** for **5.** since **6.** for **7.** since **8.** since

9 **1.** Have you seen **2.** called in **3.** is sitting in **4.** will be in charge of **5.** are **6.** chose

10 **1.** has been writing **2.** has talked **3.** has been working/has worked **4.** has just returned **5.** has always wanted **6.** has been

11 **1.** When **was** the firm established? **2.** How **did** the bank **avoid** going bankrupt? **3. Has** the company **achieved** a rise in sales this year? **4.** How many people **are missing** today? **5.** Why do half of the trainees have **to borrow** money?

12 **1.** had broken **2.** has he had **3.** have been waiting **4.** had already begun

13 **1.** will be **2.** will do **3.** am going to **4.** are going to **5.** is going to

14 **1.** is going **2.** am seeing **3.** will be sitting/am sitting **4.** will still be working **5.** arrives

15 **1.** was about to **2.** is certain to **3.** was on the verge of **4.** is due **5.** are to be **6.** is to visit

16 **1.** b **2.** a **3.** c **4.** a

Adjektive und Adverbien

1 **1.** boring **2.** confusing **3.** bored **4.** interesting **5.** excited **6.** exhausted

2 **1.** cloudy, cloudless **2.** wealthy **3.** endless **4.** joyless, joyous, joyful **5.** colourless, colourful **6.** helpless, helpful **7.** lucky, luckless **8.** dangerous

3 **1.** calm **2.** red **3.** nervous **4.** pale **5.** guilty **6.** angry **7.** awful

4 **1.** a, b **2.** b **3.** a, b **4.** b **5.** a, b

5 **1.** a **2.** c **3.** a **4.** c **5.** a **6.** a

6 **1.** nice, brown leather **2.** an old, grey business **3.** interesting, young English **4.** dirty, green plastic

7 **1.** good, better, best **2.** bad, worse, worst **3.** little, less, least **4.** old, elder, eldest
    5. much, more, most
8 **1.** enormous **2.** fantastic **3.** terrible **4.** wonderful **5.** huge   **Lösung:** unique
9 **3.** friendly ist ein Adjektiv
10 **1.** Un- **2.** ir- **3.** il- **4.** im- **5.** dis- **6.** in- **7.** un- **8.** non
11 **1.** friendly **2.** fast **3.** really **4.** equal **5.** unfairly **6.** fully
12 **1.** less **2.** Few **3.** fewer **4.** least
13 **1.** All our multi-purpose tools are manufactured for professional use. **2.** Fragile goods are wrapped
    and shipped in wooden crates. **3.** The last consignment was not insured against improper handling.
    4. The international freight forwarder we commissioned was very reliable. **5.** The new government
    has promised to increase the minimum wage.
14 **1.** as much as **2.** faster than **3.** much more experienced than **4.** not nearly/nowhere near as much
    5. slightly cheaper than **6.** hardly as efficiently as

Konditionalsätze

1 **1.** stressed out, take **2.** freezes, try **3.** don't get, tend to be **4.** is, turn on
2 **1.** drink, get **2.** doesn't return, had ... give **3.** buys, will go **4.** doesn't rain, have
    5. have, don't hesitate
3 **1.** would be **2.** store **3.** doesn't **4.** were **5.** have **6.** had
4 **1.** b **2.** g **3.** d **4.** e **5.** a **6.** c **7.** f
5 **1.** Wenn Tom zu keinem Vorstellungsgespräch eingeladen wird, wird er sich anderswo bewerben.
    2. Was würden Sie/würdest du tun, wenn Sie/du im nächsten Monat Ihre/deine Arbeit oder
    Ihren/deinen Job verlieren würden/würdest? **3.** Wäre Patricia bereit, bei Bedarf/falls erforderlich
    Überstunden zu machen? **4.** Sollte unsere Fabrik bald geschlossen werden, würden wir alle eine
    finanzielle Entschädigung bekommen.
6 **1.** didn't have to **2.** wasn't **3.** didn't always talk/wasn't always talking **4.** aren't **5.** won't have
7 **1.** a **2.** b **3.** a **4.** b **5.** a **6.** a
8 **1.** Supposing that **2.** Providing/Provided that **3.** Given that
9 **1.** identisch **2.** identisch **3.** nicht identisch
10 **1.** will have to **2.** would prefer **3.** merges **4.** establish
11 **1.** unless **2.** provided that
12 **1.** b, d **2.** c **3.** c **4.** d **5.** a, b **6.** d
13 **1.** knew **2.** had **3.** were/was **4.** could fly **5.** would earn **6.** had called/phoned

Indirekte Rede

1 **1.** was **2.** was having **3.** could do **4.** hadn't placed **5.** had been working **6.** might work
2 **1.** Past simple **2.** Past progressive **3.** Past perfect simple oder Past simple **4.** Past perfect
    progressive oder Past progressive **5.** Past perfect simple **6.** Past perfect progressive
    7. Conditional I **8.** Conditional II
3 **1.** could **2.** should/would **3.** would **4.** would have to **5.** would be able to **6.** should
4 **1.** She said she (had) closed her account because the bank had raised the charges. **2.** He said
    they expected him to pay their invoice by the end of the month. **3.** Martha said she would sign
    the contract as soon as she got it. **4.** Pete said that he was a constable and that he was sure
    he couldn't be made redundant.

5 **1.** said **2.** told **3.** said **4.** Tell **5.** tell **6.** said
6 **1.** he **2.** that/this **3.** she **4.** they **5.** they **6.** there
7 **1.** that day **2.** that night **3.** the previous day, the day before **4.** the next day, the following day
5. the following week **6.** the previous night, the night before **7.** then **8.** that
8 **1.** asked **2.** warned **3.** told **4.** begged **5.** ordered
9 **1.** c **2.** a **3.** e **4.** b **5.** h **6.** d **7.** f **8.** g
10 **1.** if **2.** where **3.** whether **4.** how **5.** if **6.** who **7.** how many **8.** whether
11 **1.** would write **2.** would start **3.** if I could tell **4.** told me to set up **5.** told me oder said to me
6. to buy **7.** was going to

Passiv

1 **1.** Passiv **2.** Aktiv **3.** Passiv **4.** Passiv **5.** Passiv **6.** Aktiv
2 **1.** was **2.** will be **3.** are **4.** have been **5.** were **6.** is being
3 **1.** acquired **2.** had just been promoted **3.** was retired **4.** had to **5.** didn't leave **6.** will be finished
4 **1.** a **2.** a, b **3.** b **4.** a, b
5 **1.** into **2.** out **3.** down **4.** into **5.** from **6.** from
6 **1.** d **2.** a **3.** b **4.** c
7 **1.** The new plant/factory will be built next year. **2.** The method was introduced in 2002 by the then
general manager. **3.** The vice president of the Belgian company has been fired. **4.** The manager is
said to have embezzled £200 000.
8 **1.** were **2.** were shown around **3.** listened **4.** were invited **5.** started **6.** went **7.** eaten
8. were served
9 **1.** is expected **2.** was rumoured **3.** believed **4.** is said
10 **1.** got stolen **2.** get tired **3.** got caught **4.** didn't get drunk **5.** is getting married **6.** got bitten
11 **1.** turned **2.** to become **3.** had gone **4.** get **5.** am growing/getting **6.** turned
12 **1.** be **2.** be **3.** have been **4.** have been

LERNKRIMI

1 **1.** destination **2.** appear **3.** promote **4.** schedule
2 **1.** with **2.** by **3.** of **4.** to **5.** of **6.** until
3 **1.** His building aggression for the moment vanishes. **2.** I do not know what to tell you.
3. We found a note in her pocket. **4.** The quickest way across the river is by ferry.
4 **1.** Did **2.** shook **3.** got **4.** was **5.** saw **6.** wore **7.** nodded **8.** said
5 **1.** b **2.** d **3.** a **4.** c
6 **1.** false, It is Ted's first week. **2.** false, They are very friendly. **3.** true **4.** false, He went to see
Marjorie's family. **5.** true

Am	amerikanisches Englisch
Br	britisches Englisch
irr	unregelmäßiges Verb/Substantiv
pl	Plural

A

A levels *Br pl*	britisches Abitur
abroad	im/ins Ausland
access	Zugang
accommodation	Unterkunft, Unterbringung
account	Konto
account holder	Kontoinhaber(in)
accountant	Buchhalter(in)
accounting, accounts	Buchhaltung
accusation	Anschuldigung
to acquire	erwerben, kaufen
to adjust	angleichen, regeln
to advertise sth.	für etw. werben
advertised	inseriert
advertisement	Anzeige, Werbung, Inserat
to advise	empfehlen, raten, mitteilen
to afford sth.	sich etw. leisten können
affordable	erschwinglich
air-conditioning	Klimaanlage
aisle	Gang
ambitious	ehrgeizig
amount	Menge
annual general meeting	Jahreshaupt-versammlung
to answer the phone	ans Telefon gehen
anwering machine	Anrufbeantworter
Any Other Business (AOB)	Sonstiges
to apologize	sich entschuldigen
apology	Entschuldigung
appalling	entsetzlich
appealing	ansprechend
application	Bewerbung
to apply	sich bewerben
appointment	Termin
to appreciate sth.	hochschätzen, dankbar sein
apprentice	Lehrling
apprenticeship	Lehre
approval	Billigung
to approve	billigen, genehmigen
area chart	Flächendiagramm
area code	Vorwahl
armchair	Sessel
to arrange	festsetzen, festlegen
as agreed	wie vereinbart
as per	laut, gemäß
as requested	wunschgemäß
as stated	wie angegeben
to ask sb. to do sth.	jmdn. bitten, etw. zu tun
to assume	annehmen, vermuten
at that	darüber hinaus
to attach	anhängen
to attend	beiwohnen, besuchen
attorney	Rechtsanwalt/-anwältin
availability	Verfügbarkeit
available	verfügbar, abkömmlich
to avert	abwenden

B

bank transfer	Banküberweisung
bankruptcy	Bankrott
bar chart	Säulendiagramm
battery	Akku
to be apprenticed *irr*	in die Lehre geschickt werden
to be based in *irr*	mit Sitz in
to be devastated *irr*	am Boden zerstört sein
to be divided on sth. *irr*	geteilter Meinung sein
to be founded in *irr*	gegründet werden in
to be in charge of *irr*	leiten, Verantwortung haben für
to be laid off *irr*	entlassen werden
to be made redundant *irr*	entlassen werden
to be much obliged *irr*	sehr zu Dank verpflichtet sein
to be on the verge/edge/brink of sth. *irr*	am Rande von etw. sein

to be trained *irr*	ausgebildet werden
bedside table	Nachttischchen
(*Am* nightstand)	
bedspread	Tagesdecke
beltway	Umgangsstraße
to bicker	streiten, zanken
bill (*Am* check)	Rechnung
blabbering	Geschwätz
blanket	(Woll)decke
blind (*Am* shade)	Rouleau
board meeting	Vorstandssitzung
body of the letter	Briefkörper
bonds *pl*	Anleihen, Renten-
	papiere
book fair	Buchmesse
to boost	hochfahren
to brace oneself for sth.	sich für etw. wappnen
breathtaking	atemberaubend
brewery	Brauerei
briefcase	Aktenkoffer,
	Aktentasche
brochure	Broschüre
building contractor	Bauunternehmer
business relations *pl*	Geschäftsbeziehungen
business trip	Geschäftsreise
by return	umgehend
bypass	Umgangsstraße

C

to call in sick	sich krank melden
to call off	absagen
cannot make sth. *irr*	nicht schaffen, nicht
	einhalten können
to cancel	absagen, stornieren
cancellation fee	Stornogebühr
to capture	einfangen
to carry sth. out	etw. durchführen
carton	Tetrapack
to cash a cheque	einen Scheck einlösen
cash register	Kasse
cashier	Kassierer(in)
cashpoint (*Am* ATM)	Geldautomat
to chair	den Vorsitz führen
change	Wechselgeld
to charge	berechnen

charger	Ladegerät
charges *pl*	Gebühren
charity organization	Wohltätigkeits-
	organisation
chart	Diagramm, Schaubild
chief executive officer	Hauptgeschäfts-
(CEO)	führer(in)
chief financial officer	Finanzchef(in)
(CFO)	
circular letter	Rundschreiben
clipboard	Klemmbrett
clogged	verstopft
closing salutation	Schlussformel
closing sentence	abschließender Satz
coffee stain	Kaffeefleck
colleague	Kollege, Kollegin
column chart	Balkendiagramm
combine	Konzern, Verband
comfirmation	Bestätigung
commissioned	beauftragt
to commute	pendeln
company	Firma
company car	Firmenwagen
compensation	Entschädigung
competitor	Konkurrent
complaint	Beschwerde
to comply with	nachkommen, erfüllen
confidence	Selbstvertrauen
confidential	vertraulich
to confirm	bestätigen
connection	Verbindung
considerably	beträchtlich
consignment	Warensendung
consultant	Berater(in)
consumer price index	Verbraucherpreisindex
contract	Vertrag
contractor	Auftragnehmer
to contradict	widersprechen
to convene	einberufen
convenience	Annehmlichkeit,
	Bequemlichkeit
convenient	günstig, passend
convention	Kongress
convertible	Cabriolet
cooperative	Genossenschaft
copier	Kopiermaschine

cordless phone	schnurloses Telefon
corporation	Kapital-/Aktien-gesellschaft
country code	Ländervorwahl
courtesy	Höflichkeit, Liebens-würdigkeit
cover letter	Begleitschreiben
crash	Unfall
crisis meeting	Krisensitzung
crossing (*Am* intersection)	Kreuzung
currently	derzeit, im Moment
curtain	Gardine
customer	Kunde, Kundin
customer complaints *irr*	Kundenbeschwerden
customer service department	Kundendienstabteilung
CV (curriculum vitae) (*Am* résumé)	Lebenslauf

D

to deal with *irr*	sich befassen/beschäftigen mit
decaf(feinated coffee)	entkoffeinierter Kaffee
to delete	löschen
to deliver	liefern
delivery date	Liefertermin
department	Abteilung
department head	Abteilungsleiter(in)
to deposit (money)	(Geld) einzahlen
desire	Wunsch, Verlangen
dessert	Nachspeise, Dessert
diary	Kalender
to differ	uneins sein, nicht einig sein
dining car (*Br* buffet compartment)	Speisewagen
direct debit	Lastschrift, Einzugs-ermächtigung
disability insurance	Erwerbsunfähigkeits-versicherung
discord	Uneinigkeit
discount	Rabatt, Preisnachlass, Skonto
to dismiss	entlassen

to dispatch	abschicken
to dissent from sth./sb.	nicht übereinstimmen mit
diversion (*Am* detour)	Umleitung
to do sport(s) *irr*	Sport treiben
dozen	Dutzend
drawing pin (*Am* thumbtack)	Reißzwecke
driving licence (*Am* driver's license)	Führerschein
to drop	fallenlassen
duvet (*Am* comforter)	Federbett

E

eletronics company	Elektronikfirma
elevator (*Br* lift)	Fahrstuhl
embarrassed	in Verlegenheit gebracht
to embezzle	veruntreuen, unterschlagen
emergency call	Notruf
emergency meeting	Dringlichkeitssitzung
to employ	beschäftigen
employee	Angestellte(r)
to enclose	beilegen, beifügen
engaged tone (*Am* busy signal)	Besetztzeichen
engaged, busy	besetzt
ensuite (bathroom)	Zimmer mit Bad
enterprise	Unternehmen
entrepreneur	Unternehmer(in)
envelope	Briefumschlag
to establish	einführen, errichten, gründen
estate car (*Am* station wagon)	Kombi
expectation	Erwartung
express letter	Eilbrief
extension (number)	Durchwahl
external hard drive	externe Festplatte

F

facilities *pl*	Einrichtung, Anlage
facility manager	Hausmeister
factory	Fabrik
to fail	unterlassen, versäumen
fair	Messe
to fall short *irr*	nicht entsprechen
fare	Fahrpreis
faulty	fehlerhaft
to feel/be under the weather *irr*	sich unwohl fühlen
to file	abspeichern, ablegen
file	Datei
filing cabinet	Aktenschrank
finance department	Finanzabteilung
financial director	Finanzleiter(in)
to fix	festsetzen
flex(i)time	Gleitzeit
folder	Aktenordner
follow-up appointment	Folgetermin
for short	kurz
foreign investments *pl*	ausländische Investitionen
fortnight	14 Tage
to forward sth.	etw. weiterleiten
forwarder	Spediteur, Spedition
four-wheel drive	Allradfahrzeug
fragile	zerbrechlich
fraud	Betrug
free of charge	kostenlos
freeze *irr*	einfrieren
freight	Fracht(gut), Güter
full-time job	Vollzeitbeschäftigung
fully booked	ausgebucht

G

gadget	Gerät, Apparat
gestures *pl*	Gesten
to get down to business *irr*	zur Sache kommen
get-together	Zusammenkunft
given that	vorausgesetzt, dass
glue stick	Klebestift

to go public *irr*	*hier:* an die Börse gehen
golden handshake	hohe Abfindung
goods *pl*	Waren
grateful	dankbar

H

to hand sth. in	etw. abgeben, einreichen
to handle	umgehen mit, handhaben
handling	Handhabung, Behandlung
hands-free phone	Freisprechanlage
to hang up on sb. *irr*	einfach auflegen
hatchback	Wagen mit Heckklappe
to have no reception *irr*	kein Netz haben
head of human resources	Personalchef(in)
head office	Hauptsitz
to hesitate	zögern
high-end	Spitzen...
to hold (the line) (*Am* to hang on) *irr*	am Apparat bleiben
hole punch	Locher
hospitality	Gastfreundschaft
to host	moderieren
hostile takeover	feindliche Übernahme
human resources (HR)	Personalabteilung
humid	schwül

I

identification	Ausweis
improper	unsachgemäß
in advance	im Voraus
in all weathers	bei jedem Wetter
in due course	zu gegebener Zeit
in favour of	zugunsten von
in response to, in reply to	als Antwort auf
in writing	schriftlich
in/with reference to	bezugnehmend auf
incentive	Anreiz, Motivation
income	Einkommen

inconvenience	Unannehmlichkeit(en)
to incur	anfallen (Kosten)
information pack	Informationsmaterial
ink cartridge	Tintenpatrone
to inquire/enquire	an-/nachfragen
inside address	Adresse des
	Empfängers
insolvency	Insolvenz, Zahlungs-
	unfähigkeit
insurance	Versicherung
insurance broker	Versicherungs-
	makler(in)
intern	Praktikant(in)
internship	Praktikum
interview	Vorstellungsgespräch
introductory discount	Einführungsrabatt
invitation	Einladung
invoice	Rechnung
to involve	zu tun haben mit
involved	verwickelt (Unfall)
to issue sth.	etw. ausgeben/
	erlassen
item	Stück, Artikel, Posten

J

job advert	Jobannonce

K

keycard	Schlüsselkarte
kitty	Kaffeekasse

L

to label	beschriften
lack	Mangel
lampshade	Lampenschirm
landline	Festnetz
lane	Fahrspur
large-scale	Groß...
to launch	auf den Markt bringen
laundry and ironing service	Wasch- und Bügelservice
leaflet	Prospekt
letter head	Briefkopf

letter of credit (L/C)	Kreditbrief
letter of intent	Absichtsschreiben
letter of recommendation	Empfehlungsschreiben
limited liability	beschränkte Haftbarkeit
limp	schlaff
line chart	Liniendiagramm
line manager	direkte(r) Vorgesetze(r)
line of business	Branche
linen	Bettwäsche
location	Standort
to log on/off	aus-/einloggen
lounge car *Am*	Salonwagen
loyalty discount	Stammkundenrabatt
luggage/baggage	Gepäck

M

main course	Hauptgericht
to make every effort *irr*	sich alle Mühe geben
to make heavy weather of sth. *irr*	etw. unnötig schwer machen
to manage	leiten, zurechtkommen
management consultant	Management- berater(in)
managing director (MD)	Generaldirektor(in)
to manufacture	herstellen
manufacturing	Herstellung
medium	medium (Steak)
menu	Speisekarte
merger	Fusion
minimum wage	Mindestlohn
minutes *pl*	Protokoll
to mistake *irr*	missverstehen, falsch verstehen
mix-up	Verwechslung
mobile (phone) (*Am* cell [phone])	Handy
motion	Antrag
mug	Kaffeebecher
muggy	schwül
multi-purpose	Mehrzweck...

N

negotiations *pl*	Verhandlungen
net	netto
net price	Nettopreis
night shift	Nachtschicht
nine-to-five job	Job mit normaler Arbeitszeit
to note	achten auf, beachten

O

objective	Ziel
offer	Angebot
to offset sth. against sth. *irr*	etw. mit etw. verrechnen
on average	im Durchschnitt
on behalf of	im Auftrag von
on request	auf Wunsch
one-way street	Einbahnstraße
open partnership	Offene Handels-gesellschaft
to operate	operieren
opportunity	günstige Gelegenheit
order	Bestellung
to order	bestellen
order number	Bestellnummer
to order sb. to do sth.	jmdm. befehlen, etw. zu tun
organization chart	Organisations-diagramm
overpass	Straßenüberführung

P

pack (of cigarettes)	(Zigaretten)päckchen
package	Paket
packaging	Verpackung
pale	blass
panorama car *Am*	Panoramawagen
parcel	Paket
parent company	Muttergesellschaft
part	Ersatzteil
to pass sth. on to sb.	jmdm. etw. weiter-leiten
to pay in (money) *irr*	(Geld) einzahlen

pay rise (*Am* pay raise) *irr*	Gehaltserhöhung
payment	Zahlung
pen	Kugelschreiber
pencil sharpener	Bleistiftspitzer
personal assistant (PA)	Persönliche(r) Assistent(in)
personal space	Höflichkeitsabstand
petrol (*Am* gas) station	Tankstelle
phone bill	Telefonrechnung
phone box (*Am* phone booth)	Telefonhäuschen
phone company	Telefongesellschaft
to pick sb. up (from swh.)	jmdn. (von irgendwo) abholen
pie chart	Tortendiagramm
pile-up	Massenkarambolage
pillow	Kopfkissen
to place an order	eine Bestellung aufgeben
(work) placement	Praktikum
placement student	Praktikant(in)
platform (*Am* track)	Bahnsteig, Gleis
posh	nobel, vornehm, schick
position	Stelle, Arbeitsplatz
post	Posten, Stelle
to post (*Am* mail) (a letter)	(einen Brief) aufgeben
postage	Porto
postal (*Am* mail) service	Postdienst
to postpone	verschieben
to pour	einschenken
to praise sb./sth. to the skies	jmdn./etw. in den Himmel loben
premises *pl*	Firmengelände, Räumlichkeiten
prestigious	renommiert
to print out	ausdrucken
printer	Drucker
private	Gefreite(r)
private limited company	GmbH
to process	bearbeiten
production manager	Produktionsleiter(in)
profound	fundiert
promising	vielversprechend

to pronounce	aussprechen	to refuse	sich weigern
to proofread *irr*	Korrektur lesen	to register (a letter)	als Einschreiben
to propose	vorschlagen		aufgeben
to provide	besorgen, liefern	registered letter/mail	Einschreiben
to provide sb. with sth.	jmdm. etw. zur	to reimburse sb. for sth.	erstatten, vergüten
	Verfügung stellen	to relaunch	erneut auf den Markt
provided/providing that	vorausgesetzt, dass		bringen
public limited company	Aktiengesellschaft	to relocate	umziehen
public phone	öffentlicher	reminder	Mahnung
	Münzfernsprecher	to remit	überweisen
public transport *Br*	öffentliche	remittance	Überweisung
	Verkehrsmittel	to renege on sth.	etw. nicht einhalten
to pull out (money) *irr*	(Geld) abheben/ziehen	rental car	Mietwagen
purchase	Kauf, Einkäufe	to report to sb.	jmdm. direkt unter-
to put in the post	in die Post geben		stellt sein
(*Am* mail) *irr*		request	Wunsch, Bitte
to put sb. on hold *irr*	jmdn. in der Warte-	requirements *pl*	Anforderungen,
	schleife halten		Bedürfnisse
to put sb. through *irr*	jmdn. durchstellen	to reschedule	neu vereinbaren
		research and	Forschung und
Q		development (R&D)	Entwicklung
		to reserve	reservieren
quarter	Quartal	responsible	verantwortlich
query	Frage	restructuring	Umstrukturierung
quilt	Steppdecke	to retire	in Rente gehen
to quit one's job	kündigen	return (*Am* round-trip)	Hin- und Rück-
quote/quotation	Kostenvoranschlag	ticket	fahrschein
		to revise	überarbeiten, ändern
R		ring road	Umgehungsstraße
		roundabout	Kreisel
to raise	erhöhen, anheben	(*Am* traffic circle)	
rally	Kundgebung	rubber (*Am* eraser)	Radiergummi
rare	englisch, blutig (Steak)	ruler	Lineal
to reach sb.	jmdn. erreichen	to run out of *irr*	ausgehen,
rear-end collision	Auffahrunfall		zu Ende gehen
to reboot	neu hochfahren		
receipt	Empfang, Erhalt		
to receive a call	einen Anruf erhalten	**S**	
receiver	(Telefon)Hörer	sales	Vertrieb
receptionist	Empfangschef/-dame	sales figures *pl*	Verkaufszahlen
to recommend	empfehlen	sales manager	Vertriebsleiter(in)
to reconsider	überdenken	sales respresentative	Vertreter(in)
to rectify	korrigieren,	sales tax *Am*	Umsatzsteuer
	berichtigen	saloon (*Am* sedan)	Limousine
reference	Betreffzeile	salutation	Begrüßungsformel
to refurbish	sanieren, renovieren	sample	Muster, Probe

to save	speichern
scenery	Landschaft
scheduled arrival	planmäßige Ankunft
scissors *pl*	Schere
screen	Bildschirm
sell-by date	Mindesthaltbarkeits-datum
sensitive	empfindlich
to set *irr*	festsetzen
to settle one's account	Rechnung bezahlen
sheet	Bettlaken
show of hands	Handzeichen
to shut down *irr*	herunterfahren
side order/dish	Beilage
signature block	Unterschriftenblock
sincere	aufrichtig
single ticket (*Am* one-way ticket)	einfache Fahrt
to sit in for sb. *irr*	jmdn. vertreten
skills *pl*	Fähigkeiten, Kenntnisse
sleeping car (*Br* sleeper)	Schlafwagen
slight change	geringfügige Änderung
slightly	geringfügig
small parcel/package	Päckchen
special meeting	Sondersitzung
to specialize in sth.	sich auf etw. spezialisieren
to specify	genau angeben
to spell *irr*	buchstabieren
to spill *irr*	verschütten
spreadsheet	Tabellenkalkulation
staff	Mitarbeiter(stab), Belegschaft
staff meeting	Belegschaftssitzung
staff member	Belegschaftsmitglied
to stage	veranstalten
stand	Messestand
standing order	Dauerauftrag
to start off with sth.	mit etw. beginnen
starter	Vorspeise
starting salary	Einstiegsgehalt
stationery	Schreibwaren
statistics *pl*	Statistik(en)
to stay	Aufenthalt
stocks *pl*	Aktien

stopover (*Am* layover)	Zwischenlandung
to store data	Daten speichern
strained	angespannt
striker	Streikende(r)
subcontractor	Zulieferfirma
subsequent	anschließend, nachfolgend
subsidiary	Tochtergesellschaft
substitute	Ersatz...
subtotal	Zwischensumme
to suit sb.	passen (Termin)
sultry	schwül
summit	Gipfel
superfluous	überflüssig
to supervise	beaufsichtigen
supplier	Lieferant
supposing (that)	gesetzt den Fall, dass
swivel chair	Drehstuhl

T

table	Tabelle
to take care of sth. *irr*	etw. erledigen
to take issue with sb. *irr*	nicht zustimmen, anderer Meinung sein
tax deduction	Steuernachlass
to tell sb. to do sth. *irr*	jmdn. auffordern, etw. zu tun
though (*nachgestellt*)	jedoch
tip	Trinkgeld
to break the news *irr*	eine Nachricht überbringen
to give the go-ahead for sth. *irr*	für etw. grünes Licht geben
to introduce sb. to sb.	jmd. jmdm. vorstellen
toll	Maut
tool	Werkzeug
total	(Gesamt)summe
trade association	Handelsgesellschaft
trade union	Gewerkschaft
traffic jam	Stau
traffic lights *pl* (*Am* stoplight[s])	Ampel
to train	ausbilden
trainee	Auszubildende(r)

training	Ausbildung
transparent film	Klarsichtfolie
travel expenses *pl*	Reisekosten, Spesen
tube ticket	U-Bahn-Ticket
to turn on/off	an-/ausmachen
turnpike *Am*	gebührenpflichtige Straße
to type	ab-/eintippen

U

underground	U-Bahn
unique	einzigartig
unless	falls/wenn nicht; es sei denn, dass
urgent	dringend

V

vice president	Vizepräsident(in)
volume discount	Mengenrabatt
vote	Wahl

W

walk-in closet	begehbarer Kleiderschrank
wardrobe	(Kleider)schrank
warehouse	Lager(haus)
to warn sb. not to do sth.	jmdn. warnen, etw. nicht zu tun
waste-paper basket	Papierkorb
to weather sth.	etw. überstehen
well-done	gut durch (Steak)
wholesale discount	Großhandelsrabatt
wi-fi	WLAN
wine list	Getränkekarte
to withdraw (money) *irr*	(Geld) abheben/ziehen
within walking distance	in Fußnähe/fußläufig
wooden crate	Holzkiste
to work from home	von zu Hause arbeiten
to work overtime	Überstunden machen
to work part-time	halbtags arbeiten
workplace	Arbeitsplatz
to wrap sth. in	etw. einwickeln

Sprachtraining Englisch
Übung macht den Meister!

144 Seiten
ISBN 978-3-8174-1764-3

Das Übungsbuch ist ideal für geübte Anfänger und Lerner mit mittlerem Sprachniveau, die ihre Englischkenntnisse auffrischen und vertiefen möchten. Rund 200 thematisch sortierte Übungen zu Wortschatz und Grammatik machen das Training abwechslungsreich und effektiv.

Infokästen erklären sprachliche und landeskundliche Besonderheiten. Lösungen und Glossar im Anhang.

Extra: Krimilektüre für geübte Anfänger – so wird das Sprachtraining noch spannender!

Auch für Niveau A1-A2 erhältlich:
144 Seiten
ISBN 978-3-8174-1648-6